# CARING FOR SOCIETY

## A Theological Interpretation
## of Lay Ministry

# CARING FOR SOCIETY

## A Theological Interpretation of Lay Ministry

### Robert L. Kinast

### THE THOMAS MORE PRESS
Chicago, Illinois

ISBN 0-88347-197-3

# CONTENTS

*Introduction*

    John Henry Newman    7
    Catholic Action    8
    Yves Congar    10
    Vatican II    12
    Purpose of the Book    13

*Chapter One:* The Experience

    Categories of Lay Activity    17
        Voluntary Activity    17
        Church Professional Activity    21
        Societal Activity    25
        Dutiful Activity    28
        Independent Activity    30
    The Interpretations    33
        Yves Congar    34
        Leonard Doohan    36
        Chicago Declaration    38
        Called and Gifted    40
    Value of Ministry in the World    44
        Role of the Clergy    45
        Role of Spirituality    46
        Role of Community    46

*Chapter Two:* The Dominant Factor: Lay Ministry

    Scope of the Term    49
    Relationships    51
    Preparation-Recognition    57
    Meaning of Lay Ministry    59

*Chapter Three:* The Contrasting Factors

    Laity-Clergy Relations    66
      History    67
      Theology    72
      Praxis    79
    World-Church Relations    84
      Vatican II    84
      The Secularity of the Laity    89
      Secularizing of the Clergy    92

*Chapter Four:* Symbolization: The Care of Society

    Pastoral Care    96
    Care of Society    101
    The Care of Society as Lay Ministry    111

*Chapter Five:* Enactment

    Love of the World    119
    Lay Authority    131
    Spirituality of Engagement    141
    Occasion-Centered Community    151

*Notes,*    159

# INTRODUCTION

In the hierarchy alone reside the right and authority of moving and directing the members toward the established goal of the society, whereas it is the duty of the multitude to let itself be governed and to follow obediently the lead of its directors.[1]

POPE PIUS X wrote these words in his 1906 encyclical, *Vehementer Nos.* They have frequently been paraphrased as "the only duty of the laity is to pray, pay, and obey." Both the papal and the popular version seem out of place today. In order to understand why, it is helpful to take a brief historical look at recent developments.

## *John Henry Newman*[2]

Almost fifty years before Pius X's encyclical, John Henry Newman had asserted that the laity should be consulted in the process of formulating church doctrine. He cited the dogmatic definition of the Immaculate Conception (in 1850) as an actual example of this and urged that the same attention be given to the laity in practical matters as well. There was considerable disagreement with this view.

So Newman drew upon his extensive knowledge of the early church and skillfully invoked the authority of the widely respected Vatican theologian, Fr. Perrone, to show that the laity had better preserved belief in Jesus' divinity against the fourth century Arians than the hierarchy had. This and other instances led him to affirm that the "sense of the faithful" is a source and norm of doctrinal truth which the church bypasses at its own peril.

Newman's essay stimulated a renewed appreciation of the laity; it accented their active and positive contribution to the life and teaching of the church. This view did not gain immediate or widespread acceptance, however, as evidenced by the quote from Pope Pius X above. But as often happens, external circumstances prompt change within the church when internal forces cannot.

Events in the history of modern Europe signaled a steady decline in the direct influence of the Roman Catholic church on society. Industrial, political, and humanistic revolutions were leaving the institutional church in an isolated position. The clergy and religious had very little direct impact on the development of life on the continent. In such straits a new appeal was made to the laity in the name of Catholic Action.

### Catholic Action[3]

From the beginning, Catholic Action was hierarchically inspired, defined, and controlled. The major impetus for the Catholic Action movement came from Pope Pius XI. Claiming to have received an inspiration one Pentecost Sunday, Pius XI issued a call to the Catholic laity "to participate in the apostolate of the hierarchy." For the next quarter century Catholic Action was the primary vehicle through which lay activity was defined and organized.

The Catholic Action movement reflected the hierarchical-institutional model of church which dominated almost everyone's thinking at that time. In such a church there could be no greater honor than to be invited, by its head, to share in the work of the hierarchy. There was some difference of opinion, however, about how far this sharing extended.

Some held that it included a share in the hierarchical power of orders, or at least in the power of jurisdiction. Most commentators, however, argued that the laity's participation always remained dependent on the hierarchy and therefore could not include a share in the actual power of jurisdiction or of orders.

Pius XII tried to clarify matters by reformulating the definition of Catholic Action to say that the laity "collaborate" in the apostolate of the hierarchy. This resolved the question of powers but other questions remained. Did everything lay Catholics do fall under Catholic Action? What about existing lay organizations such as the Legion of Mary and the special case of secular institutes? What was the primary focus of Catholic Action: formation of its own members to be better Christians or activity to change society and make it more amenable to Christianity?

In the course of answering these questions, a consensus emerged which included the following points. (1) Catholic Action as a term has a broad and a specific meaning. The broad meaning refers to all the apostolic activities of the laity, whether organized or not, which flow from the fundamental commitment of baptism. In this sense Catholic Action is as ancient as Christianity itself, a point frequently stressed by the popes. The specific meaning of Catholic Action refers to that *form* of lay activity which is mandated by the hierarchy and which is therefore accountable to the hierarchy. This formal aspect is the distinctive characteristic of Catholic Action as initiated by Pius XI.

(2) Catholic Action has two primary goals: the spiritual-moral-theological formation of its members and the spreading of Christ's Kingdom in the world. The two are inseparable. The action goal is to spread the Kingdom but

this can't be done authentically without adequate personal formation. On the other hand, a purely pious organization of lay persons with no apostolic purpose would not fit the definition of Catholic Action.

(3) Catholic Action underscored the conviction that the church's mission includes the world. Catholic Action was organized precisely because the salvation of the world was of prime concern and was seen as an integral part of the church's total mission. The limited impact on society by the hierarchy helped to accentuate the special opportunity and responsibility of the laity. This social mission did not have to be carried out in the specific form of Catholic Action, but it did have to be carried out.

Despite a great deal of attention, discussion, organization, and energy, Catholic Action never seemed to mobilize the majority of the laity. It remained something of an elite movement, and it appealed primarily to lay persons already committed to a hierarchical church. Nonetheless, Catholic Action did give positive emphasis to the laity and affirmed their active role in the mission of the church. No major change could occur, however, until the understanding of the church itself would shift. And this began to happen after World War II.

### Yves Congar[4]

Near the height of Catholic Action but before the first stirrings of Vatican II a new understanding of church began to emerge. One of its chief proponents was the French Dominican, Yves Congar. In 1954 Congar published a major work entitled, *Lay People in the Church*. It was really an ecclesiology with the focus on the laity. Congar himself insisted that the only adequate theology of the laity would be a total ecclesiology.

Congar did not claim to produce such a total ecclesiology, but he did try to interpret the role of the laity in the church in positive and active terms. He did this primarily in two ways. First, he affirmed the secularity of the laity as a positive contribution to the life and mission of the church. As Christian believers who deal with created, worldly things, the laity underscore the rightful autonomy of the created order and prevent it from being absorbed into a world-denying mentality.

At the same time, because the laity share with the clergy and religious the one call to holiness, they keep the world oriented toward God's ultimate purpose which is symbolized as the Kingdom of God. Thus the world, the church, and the Kingdom of God are all related. The laity's gift is to affirm the world and keep it related to the Kingdom.

The second way Congar stressed the positive role of the laity was to spell out how the laity share in the threefold work of Christ as priest, prophet, and pastor. In each of the three offices Congar showed that the laity's participation was more inclusive and more permanent than the clergy's. It was more inclusive because the laity were identified by baptism with the most fundamental meaning of Christ's priestly, prophetic, and ruling role. The clergy by ordination have a more specialized and therefore more limited participation.

For example, Congar defines priesthood in terms of sacrifice and characterizes sacrifice primarily as putting oneself in a right relation toward another, ultimately God. From this fundamental meaning, outward expressions of true sacrifice, including the cultic expression, follow. When this is elaborated, it is clear that ordained priesthood is a small part of the total meaning of priesthood. This small part has a qualitative excellence, which Congar upholds, but it is properly understood only when it is located in the larger context of the priesthood which is shared by all the faithful.

The laity's participation in the priesthood of Christ is also more permanent than the clergy's. The cultic and hierarchical priesthood are part of the divine economy established in this world. As such, they will pass away, but the more fundamental participation in Christ's priesthood is eternal. This does not mean that clergy are left out but rather that their specialized participation is temporary. Congar used this same pattern to interpret the laity's participation in the kingly, prophetic, and apostolic functions of the church as well as its communal life and holiness.

These observations represented a fresh approach to the dignity and role of the laity in the church. They were complemented by the writings of other theologians who became the prime contributors to discussions on the laity when the Second Vatican Council convened.

## Vatican II[5]

When Pope John XXIII summoned the Second Vatican Council, he had a dual purpose in mind: to renew the life of the church in head and members with a deliberate thrust toward Christian unity and to contribute more effectively to developments in the modern world. These were, of course, the basic goals of Catholic Action. The Council gave that movement a unique opportunity to influence the life of the church in the world. But in the course of the Council an unexpected shift in the understanding of the church occurred which reshaped the understanding and role of the laity.

Thanks to the groundwork of theologians like Congar, a

more holistic ecclesiology emerged, symbolized by the image of the People of God. The Council began to rethink everything in light of the church as the People of God. This concept made any exaggerated distinction between clergy and laity obsolete.

The final documents of the Council were a typical mixture of tradition and novelty, prophecy and compromise. They do not present a completely coherent picture of the laity. The major, explicit treatments of the laity are found in chapter four of the Constitution on the Church and, of course, the entire Decree on the Apostolate of the Laity. Substantial discussion of the role of the laity is also included in the Pastoral Constitution on the Church in the Modern World, the Decree on the Church's Missionary Activity, the Declaration on Christian Education, and the Declaration on Religious Freedom. In short, the laity permeate the documents of Vatican II.

But more important than documents is experience. In its documents Vatican II tried to summarize and affirm the experience of the laity up to that time. But the Council itself gave birth to a new experience which continues to be developed by lay persons today. That experience is the starting point of this book.

### Purpose of the Book

I approach the experience of the laity since the Second Vatican Council as a theologian. My intention is best expressed by the authors of the book *Parish, Priest, People.*[6]

> Rather than trying to place an existing model of ministry on top of the laity we might better assume that lay Catholics are acting out a ministry experientially, and

our task is to discover the key elements in that experience and help people to articulate them within a framework consonant with the Christian tradition.

This book is my attempt to articulate the experience of the laity in a framework consonant with the Christian tradition.

To do this requires a model for theologizing from experience. The model I will use consists of five sequential steps.[7]

### 1. *Experience*

The first step is to gather the experience. For purposes of this book the experience is limited to Catholic laity in the United States since Vatican II. This is still a vast field of experience. It is impossible to assemble it comprehensively. My hope is to represent it adequately. This will be done in two parts. The first summarizes the main types of lay activity; the second examines recent theological interpretations of that activity. This material constitutes chapter one.

### 2. *Dominant Factor*

Formal theological interpretation begins by identifying the dominant factor within the field of experience gathered in chapter one. From my perspective lay ministry is the dominant factor in the experience of the laity since Vatican II. This will be presented in chapter two.

### 3. *Contrasting Factor*

The meaning of lay ministry is amplified by identifying the chief contrasting factors which define the reality of lay ministry. There are two such factors: lay-clergy relations and world-church relations. Both will be discussed in chapter three.

### 4. *Symbolization*

The next step in this model of theological interpretation is to symbolize the investigation of chapters one, two, and three. The role of a symbol in this regard is to bring the material together in a way that opens up new possibilities. I will suggest the symbol of "the care of society" and develop its meaning in chapter four.

### 5. *Enactment*

The final step is to put the results of this reflection process into action. This, of course, goes beyond the capacity of a book. However, some of the practical implications of enacting the symbol, the care of society, will be described. This will constitute chapter five.

In this model chapters one to three are analytical and draw upon knowledge that is already available. Step four is imaginative. It pushes toward a new insight. Step five is really a new experience but in continuity with the originating experience, at least in the sense that the enactment proposed results from a careful interpretation of the experience originally given.

How accurate or useful this interpretation is remains for the reader to say. I offer it in the same spirit as the U.S. Catholic bishops when they reflected on the experience of the laity in their 1980 statement, *Called and Gifted:*

> We are convinced that the laity are making an indispensible contribution to the experience of the People of God and that the full import of their contributions is still in a beginning form in the post-Vatican II church. We have spoken in order to listen.[8]

# CHAPTER ONE

## *The Experience*[1]

THE experience of the Catholic laity since the Second Vatican Council is vast. Although much of this experience has been recorded or included in surveys, studies, conferences, reports, books, or newsletters, a great deal more remains in the untold stories of lay persons. Nonetheless, what has been gathered is impressive, even overwhelming.

The purpose of this chapter is to present a relatively adequate description of the experience of the Catholic laity. This will be done in two parts. The first will describe lay activity, using five broad categories. These are not scientific categories. They serve only to direct attention to the typical patterns of lay activity since Vatican II. It is hoped that this description will ring true to the experience of the reader.

The categories are voluntary, church professional, societal, dutiful, and independent lay activity. In each category I shall describe in general what is meant, give some indication of who belongs, and then suggest what contribution that particular activity makes to a comprehensive view of the laity in the United States.

The second part of the chapter will review four theological interpretations of lay activity since Vatican II. The focus is on theological interpretations because that is the main interest of this book. These theological interpretations will be combined with the descriptions of lay activity presented in part one of this chapter to set the stage for my own theological interpretation beginning in chapter two.

## CATEGORIES OF LAY ACTIVITY

### Voluntary Activity[2]

Voluntary activity is the work of lay persons who willingly contribute their time, enthusiasm, skill, resources, and influence to activities sponsored by the church. This activity usually takes place in a parish setting. Volunteers are the persons who make the postconciliar parishes work. They have different degrees of availability and commitment and a wide variety of special interests.

The most observable area of voluntary activity has been the liturgy. In addition to the traditional services of sanctuary care, ushering, and music leadership, lay persons now regularly read the Scripture lessons and assist with the distribution of communion (including in many places taking communion to the sick). Lay persons do all this without being formally installed in these liturgical ministries.

Women usually have equal access with men to these roles. The glaring exception to this is the permanent diaconate which is restricted to men. The diaconate itself is an ambiguous instance of lay activity because it is part of the sacrament of orders but is exercised by men who are in every other respect lay persons. To the degree they are perceived as lay persons, permanent deacons extend liturgical lay activity to the roles of preaching, baptizing formally, and witnessing sacramental marriages.

These visible activities are complemented by a still greater range of opportunities which lay persons have for planning liturgical functions, coordinating these with other events in the parish especially religious education programs, training liturgical ministers, and implementing sound liturgical principles. Virtually every aspect of the

preparation and celebration of liturgical events is open to
lay persons with the exception of those roles reserved to ordained ministers.

One of the primary vehicles for this liturgical involvement has been the liturgy committee. The liturgy committee is part of an expanded committee system which has
emerged in parishes and dioceses since Vatican II. Committees of lay persons were in operation before Vatican II,
of course. This was especially true with regard to building
and maintenance (sometimes including finance and bud-
get), social activities within the church, charitable works
(such as St. Vincent de Paul), devotional and pious services
(such as Sodalities, Legion of Mary, Holy Name), youth
activities (mostly CYO), and education both in parochial
schools and C.C.D. classes.

After Vatican II these committees sometimes expanded
their functions and sometimes expanded their influence.
Charitable organizations often developed into peace and
justice groups, with a strong emphasis on changing social
systems and a critical awareness of the need for structural
change. This has been most evident with the issue of abortion and more recently nuclear arms.

Social activities within the church took on the character
of "community building" and were sometimes linked to
outreach programs with an ecumenical or evangelization
thrust. And education underwent a major transformation
as the focus shifted from parochial schools to religious
education, including special programs for youth, families,
and adults.

One of the committee structures that is relatively new
since Vatican II is the parish council. Conceived as a practical implementation of Vatican II's emphasis on shared
responsibility, parish councils have had a mixed history.
On the one hand, they do provide an opportunity for lay

representation and leadership in the life of the parish. On the other hand, the degree of actual influence lay persons can exert through parish councils depends almost entirely on the particular pastor. And pastors usually retain ultimate decision-making power so that parish councils are essentially consultative.

This has been a source of frustration to many lay persons who expected to have more authority in making parish decisions. This expectation has sometimes been fueled by contact with other Christian churches who give the laity a much greater voice in church affairs. On the other hand, many pastors who sincerely want to involve the laity in the church experience their own frustrations.

One is the simple lack of competence to work effectively with groups. The skills needed to delegate tasks, reinforce volunteers, achieve consensus, resolve conflict, manage time, set objectives, evaluate progress were not taught to many pastors when they were in seminary. Without the necessary skills, pastors could have bad experiences with parish councils and get soured on the whole idea.

Compounding this frustration was the discovery that many lay persons did not want to share responsibility for the parish, while those who did sometimes had their own agenda to propagate and were not all that desirable in leadership roles.

The initial disappointment of laity and clergy alike with parish councils has given rise to a concerted effort to clarify the function of such groups and to acquire the skills needed to run them effectively. The learnings derived from this effort are transferable to other committees and groups. As a result there is a gradual increase in the competencies required to make the postconciliar structure work effectively.

Most of the parish committees have a diocesan counterpart and many have a regional or national structure as well. The same problems encountered with parish committees appear on the diocesan level with the additional difficulty of generating a sense of ownership of the diocese among lay persons whose faith life is primarily parish centered.

On the other side, lay representatives to diocesan committees often experience difficulty sharing their experience at the parochial level while trying to arouse parochial interest (of both laity and clergy) in diocesan projects and concerns. All this is epitomized by the struggling existence of diocesan pastoral councils and the reluctance to form a national pastoral council.

In addition to the numerous committees which have been formed as part of the official structure of the parish or diocese, there are also many groups, organizations, and activities which lay persons have initiated on their own. These have often had a prayer or spiritual development or adult education or social service thrust. It is hard to gather information about them because they are informal and do not appear in published listings or resource guides. Finally, there are lay persons who are paid for their services but who work for the church primarily because they want to help. This is evidenced by the many secretaries, administrative assistants, program coordinators, bookkeepers, housekeepers, and janitors who accept low salaries and benefits and heavy work schedules.

On the whole the contribution of volunteers is to carry the renewal of Vatican II into action. But volunteers are vulnerable. They are easily taken for granted, especially if they are dependable and efficient and seek no recognition. By comparison with full-time, professionally trained staff, especially priests and sisters, volunteers often acquire a subordinate status whether anyone intends it or not. The rest of a volunteer's responsibilities and commitments to family, work, neighborhood, friends, and leisure are over-looked by those whose concern is for the parish task to be done and the volunteers needed to do it.

Sometimes this means that volunteers are asked to do boring, menial, time-consuming work when they have more valuable contributions to make. Or they may be quite willing to do these things, but they do not want to be taken for granted or have it assumed that they are available for "whatever" those in charge want done.

There is another side to the volunteer's vulnerability. Sometimes a person volunteers and discovers that there is no direction or support coming from the parish staff. In the name of "enabling" or "facilitating" the use of people's gifts, staff members may in fact abdicate their proper leadership or direction-giving role. This places an unfair burden of responsibility on the volunteer.

Despite this vulnerability, volunteers do not appear to be declining. They are exerting a positive and renewing influence on the church, especially at the parish level. Their volunteerism affirms the value of the church and the organized Christian life. Taking advantage of new opportunities, volunteers manifest just how diverse and richly gifted the People of God is.

At the same time volunteers tend to find their place and help maintain the existing system of church life. They reinforce the values expressed by the system they volunteer to keep going. Within that context they exhibit great good will, competence, spirit, and worth. They give the church energy and stability.

## Church Professional Activity[3]

The most striking new development in lay activity since Vatican II has been the emergence of professionally trained lay ministers. This development has been fed by two sources in particular: the sharp decline in the number of priests and sisters in the postconciliar church and the increase in the range of services needed to implement the renewal of Vatican II. Bishops and priests tend to cite the first factor when encouraging professional lay ministers, but the second factor is the primary motivation for the lay men and women themselves.

The decline in the number of priests and sisters has resulted in a shortage of personnel to staff the existing structure of church life. This situation (a crisis to many) is not going to change, so it provides an occasion for considering alternatives. However, there has been very little official movement in this direction. Regarding ordained ministry alone, celibacy remains an irremovable requirement and women remain unacceptable candidates. These are not the only factors contributing to the overall shortage of ordained ministers, but they are the most noteworthy and the ones over which the official church has most control.

Although the number of priests has declined, the number of parishes and parishioners has not declined in the same ratio. In fact the American Catholic parish appears to be quite strong on the whole. This has led bishops to seek ways to strengthen the basic territorial structure of the parish. While vacancies caused by a decline in the number of priests remain in the postconciliar parish, new positions are being created as the church enters more and more fully into the renewal launched by Vatican II.

To fill both the traditional and the new positions, lay persons have been acquiring professional training in ministry, theology, and related fields. Most of them study in Protestant seminaries or schools of theology, although there is some opportunity to study in various Catholic seminaries along with candidates for ordination.

Rarely do these lay persons have any job guarantee while they study, nor are they sponsored by a diocese or religious community as seminarians are. Rather they complete their training (usually a Master of Divinity degree) and then seek employment as church ministers. If jobs are available, one of the next and most difficult problems is salary. Wages are generally scaled to priests and sisters. Even with the increases for these church workers in recent years, many professional lay ministers, especially with families, find such wages and related benefits are not enough to live on.

In addition, there is a larger and less tangible matter of job satisfaction and acceptance by the primary professionals in ministry—the priests. Although they are trained to do pastoral care and counseling, to preach and lead groups, professional lay ministers may be able to find work only as directors of religious education or youth directors or liturgy organizers. These are not insignificant roles, of course, but often a lay minister is trained and eager to do other services.

But even when they can do pastoral care, they are limited in the range of sacramental ministry they can offer, especially when unable to anoint the ill persons they have cared for, to absolve sacramentally those they have counseled, to witness officially the marriage of those they have prepared. In many instances the preparation exceeds the actual ministry which they can perform.

Acceptance as peers in the ministry is another problem. Some clergy look upon professional lay ministers as interim helpers, necessitated by the current crisis but not really equal partners or fully contributing co-ministers. If all else were equal, a priest would always be preferable.

In addition, professional lay ministry *is* an alternative to priesthood and perhaps a more attractive one to young people. This fact is threatening to some priests and may inadvertently weaken their own shaky identity or confidence. Such feelings may not be very widespread or overt, but wherever they exist they contribute to a climate that is not productive of good ministry.

Professional lay ministers are not the only ones to experience this, of course. Permanent deacons have encountered the same attitudes, as did sisters when they began getting active in a variety of ministries and were not limited to hospital and school work. Undoubtedly, sisters faced even stronger resentment because they were women moving into the male domain. Professional lay women can therefore expect to face a double burden.

The persistence of "new" ministers and the responsiveness of many priests is gradually reshaping the pattern of professional ministry in the church, but there is still a long way to go. Two of the most important areas for improvement are spirituality and community. Both are vital to a healthy ministry and both are yearned for by professional lay ministers. This is true during ministerial preparation as well as during ministerial practice. There is a feeling of being abandoned, or at least of not being included, in the shared prayer life and community experience of full-time, ordained ministers. Of course, one may question how vital and genuine the spirituality and community experience actually is among priests (and sisters), but to whatever degree it exists, professional lay ministers find that they are routinely, even if unintentionally, segregated from it. The feeling of isolation and even rejection is hard to overcome.

Despite these and other obstacles, professional lay ministers continue to grow in numbers and make their contribution. They represent to some degree an alternative to ordination and vowed community life. They sense a deep desire to serve the Lord and the church, but they see more options than priesthood or religious communities. For young persons especially who are choosing their careers and planning their families, this is a courageous and pioneering undertaking.

Professional lay ministers appear to be a solid addition to the structure of the church in the U.S. Especially as they create new roles and introduce new claims to leadership, they will help reshape the church system. And for those who do not stay in formal church ministry or who cannot find suitable work there, they can bring to secular occupations a new level of theological and ministerial competence. If this were to happen, it would represent a unique fulfillment of the original intent of Catholic Action and would also connect with the next type of lay activity.

### Societal Activity[4]

The rapid increase in the number and types of service within the church, both for volunteers and professionals, has been paralleled by the occasions for Christian service in the world. These are not as easily categorized because they permeate modern social life and are more numerous and more complex than the activities which take place within the specific confines of the church.

The social area, of course, has long been targeted as the special sphere of activity for lay persons. Prior to Vatican II this was stressed in a formal way through Catholic Action. After Vatican II the same social thrust has been strengthened in two important ways.

First of all, the growing body of social teaching authored by Leo XIII, Pius XI, Pius XII, and John XXIII received a forceful reaffirmation at the Council. The church's relation to the modern world was the topic of an entire document while the pressing social issue of religious liberty was given a new interpretation. Other explicit social themes were addressed while the principles and foundations of the church's social involvement were touched upon in sections of other documents.

After the Council, there has been a continual emphasis on the social mission of the church expressed at every level of the church. There have been additional papal encyclicals by Paul VI and John Paul II and pronouncements in connection with papal visits. The 1971 Synod of Bishops issued a strong statement on social justice; national conferences of bishops have addressed similar issues, the most widely publicized being those of the Latin American bishops and the recent statement of the U.S. bishops on peace and nuclear weapons.

Conferences of religious superiors and religious communities have taken bold stands on many issues and backed them up with concrete actions. All this official church input has kept alive the importance of social justice and has also continually tried to clarify issues and offer direction for action.

How effective this has been in promoting lay involvement is hard to say. But by comparison with the preconciliar state of affairs, there is a remarkable, extensive literature which feeds the social mission of the church.

The second factor which has influenced the social thrust of the church has been the stream of major social crises since the Council ended and the deluge of information about them. Beginning with the war in southeast Asia and the black civil-rights movement in the mid-1960s, the postconciliar church in the U.S. has been confronted by challenges of nuclear power and defense, women's rights, a new economic order, immigration, ecology, racism, crime, drugs, corruption in government. . . .

The interconnection of all these issues and a heightening consciousness of how they affect us have intensified the need to respond in a Christian way and to do so precisely in the public forum of society.

Undeniably those lay persons included in categories one and two above have made some response in and through the church. But there are others who make the primary expression of their Christian life a social commitment. They may exert their influence through church-related activities and groups (such as peace and justice committees) or independently of any such explicit connection (such as the League of Women Voters or Common Cause). In either case these lay persons tend to be active members of parishes or campus communities or other intentional faith groups. They may participate to some degree in the internal activities of their faith communities, but they channel their energies and talents primarily toward social action rather than the maintenance and development of church life and structures.

Sometimes there is tension between lay persons with this orientation and the church volunteers and professionals. Feelings of competition can arise because there are only so many resources, so much energy, and so much attention that can be devoted to good causes whether ecclesial or societal. Judgments can be made about the motives and authenticity of someone's involvement in church work when their help is desired in societal work (and the reverse is also true).

Despite the amount of social teaching and the critical nature of social issues, there seems to be greater response to opportunities for lay service within the church. The societal dimension of the church's mission and the special contribution of lay persons to that mission remains by and large underdeveloped. As a result lay persons committed to societal activity often go about their service in relative anonymity. This can easily lead to feelings of isolation and even alienation when the church in its public behavior seems to highlight its own needs and programs.

These feelings are confirmed at times by the particular issues one advocates. Whereas right to life and nuclear disarmament have highly visible support from the official church, women's rights, criminal justice, foreign policy, ecology, government legislation do not enjoy the same degree of support.

Thus, lay persons who engage in societal activity experience a double burden in making their contribution. They take on complex and controversial issues in a pluralistic society and they do so as members of a church which gives ambivalent support to their priority. These societal lay persons are inevitably in tension with both society and church. They confront society with values that are increasingly countercultural, and they confront the church with priorities that alter the present emphasis on internal church life. Those who can take up this dual challenge will probably never be very numerous. They are the edge, the tension, the prophetic push that both society and the church need. Their contributions may be perceived as unwelcome, but they are indispensible for both institutions.

### Dutiful Activity[5]

The largest number of lay persons are the least active. They are dutiful Catholics. These are women and men who attend church regularly, support the church financially, identify themselves as Catholics on records and forms, but are not actively involved in planning and leadership roles. They often feel that all they can do is fulfill their family and work responsibilities. They ask only for occasional or special services from the church like baptism, marriage, education, or support in times of crisis.

Dutiful activity means such lay persons are willing to do what is expected in order to be good Catholics. They look to church authorities (priests, sisters, staff) to declare these expectations. This fosters a type of willing dependency which church authorities, especially those who like or need to be depended upon, respond to. Dutiful laity see themselves as members, as the rank and file, the supporters of the church. They don't really see themselves *as* church. They have made the changes since Vatican II, but they are not necessarily changed.

It is hard to know just how the Catholic value system and way of life really influences their decisions and lifestyle. An easy separation between church and life is possible for dutiful laity because they remain essentially private believers. Unlike the laity in category three who forge connections between Christian values and societal life, dutiful laity evidence no special integration or need of it.

Many do, however, maintain a certain piety and cultural affinity with Catholicism. This is true especially for persons who were raised before the Council, but it is also found among younger Catholics who are rediscovering what their parents and grandparents may have discarded (or had taken away from them). The primary goal of dutiful Catholics is their own salvation. Progress in this regard is measured largely by the approval of the official church which reinforces the tendency toward dutifulness.

Dutiful laity are not necessarily conservative or traditionalist in their behavior and conviction about other things, but they do tend to be traditional in their attitude and feeling-for membership in the church. They are the

Catholic representatives of a religious culture which may have more to do with culture and broadly accepted religious values than with the specific claims of the Christian gospel as interpreted in the Catholic tradition.

Dutiful Catholics don't raise many questions and aren't attracted to the debates and tensions within the church. They have personal views on many issues but don't express them publicly and don't seek discussion of them. They are content to let public issues be governed by current church order; the rest (perhaps most) remains private.

Like volunteers, dutiful laity contribute to the stability and support of the church in its existing institutional aspect. They are something like a silent majority who receive and appreciate the services offered by the church through the clergy and active lay leaders.

### Independent Activity[6]

The term most often used to describe lay persons in this group is "the unchurched." This term draws attention to those lay persons who no longer participate in established church systems, and it carries a built-in bias toward active church membership as the criterion for Christian living.

But labeling people as unchurched does not necessarily address the reasons why persons are no longer affiliated as they once were, nor does it indicate what their current experience is. The term independent, therefore, is meant to say that persons have made a decision and as a result of it they experience themselves as independent (of church structure). The decision may stem from disagreement with certain church teachings (e.g., on artificial contraception, abortion, celibacy) or church practice (e.g., restriction of women's roles or prohibition of remarriage by divorced

Christians) or attitudes (e.g., lack of support for social issues, a desire to exert control).

Sometimes the decision is bound up with a life stage to which the church seems to have little to contribute. Independent laity sense it is time to move on. For still others independent activity is a way to cope with church burnout.

There is also a group of lay persons who do not so much leave the church in a deliberate act but just stop going or drift away. Perhaps there was never much to hold them in the first place. At some point they just seem to ease out of the conditioning and behaviors associated with belonging actively to the church. It is dubious how independent they are, because they may have no significant relation to Christianity at all.

The widespread impression is that many now independent persons might reconsider their status if they were reached and invited back to the church. A part of the current evangelization effort is aimed at the unchurched who are perceived as in fact dropouts. A central strategy in this effort is lay-to-lay or peer-to-peer outreach. The assumption is that active lay persons may get a better hearing than priests and sisters who are too easily identified with the problems that may have initially led persons to take a more independent turn.

It is hard to say how effective this outreach is or can be. In some places programs to welcome back former Catholics have been successful, at least in reactivating persons in church life. The sincerity and openness of active lay persons create a good feeling and offer the possibility of returning gracefully.

Another dimension of this outreach effort which is generally not pursued is to elicit from independent laity the reasons why they initially left. An honest dialogue on this point could provide church leaders with valuable insights and suggestions regarding the ongoing renewal of the church. The difficulty, of course, is to identify such persons and let them tell their stories.

The chief contribution of these independent lay persons is an alternative in practice to the customary forms of Catholic life. As persons who were once members of the organized church and still maintain an intentional, Christian way of life, they challenge the existing church system to open its definition and criteria for being Chrisian. Are they in or out of the church? Such questions will inevitably arise and pose a new opportunity to rethink the issue of membership and indeed the very nature of church. They have another type of experience to share, one that stretches the existing order to be sure. Because they are independent, they cannot be included easily in existing categories; but because they are also Christians, they cannot be simply disregarded.

*Summary*

As mentioned at the outset, these are not scientific categories. They are largely impressionistic, and they are not exhaustive. Many experiences of lay persons cannot be conveniently placed within these descriptions. But they do represent one way of assembling the great diversity which constitutes the lay experience in the U.S. after Vatican II.

Taken as a whole, the experience seems to be that lay persons are still mostly identified with the parish structure. Even when there are other primary involvements (as in number three, societal activity), the parish remains an integral part of the person's lifestyle.

The bulk of activity is done by persons who are not

employed by the church (volunteers) and do not identify professionally with it, although there is a significant rise in the number of trained lay persons for professional church service. The most attention and support has gone to church-related activity, although the traditional arena for lay activity is society and there has been a consistent outpouring of church teachings on social issues.

The lay experience covers a full range of attitudes and feelings toward the church, extending from active commitment and involvement in church life to the same degree of involvement in society. These active laity are couched among the dutiful, with independent laity framing the whole.

## THE INTERPRETATIONS

The experience of the laity since Vatican II has given rise to various interpretations. Some have come from the laity themselves and some have come from clergy. In this section I want to examine four representative reflections on the laity. Together they encompass most of the discussion which has been going on and will serve as a framework for noting significant points.

Before turning to these representative interpretations, I want to make a few preliminary observations on the literature which has appeared in the U.S. on the topic of the laity. The first thing to note is a decline in the sheer number of articles and books which explicitly discuss the laity. Part of the explanation for this is that pertinent themes are now treated under other categories like church, ministry, social action. Nonetheless, cross references indicate that fewer essays deal with laity topics than before and during the Council.

A second observation is that the term Catholic Action, and interest in it, disappeared almost immediately after the Council. Other terms like lay apostolate or lay-clergy relations continued to receive a lot of attention, but Catholic Action simply ceased to be a context for discussion of the laity after Vatican II.

A third significant observation is that a new category was introduced in volume 19 of the Guide to Catholic Periodical Literature (covering the years 1977-1978). That category is "Lay Ministry." The number of articles in this category has steadily grown.

A final symbolic note. If one were to check for material on lay-clergy relations, one would be referred to the heading, clergy-lay relations. Obviously, the alphabetical listing is the reason why, but symbolically this order also indicates the priority which many lay persons experience.

### Yves Congar[7]

The first representative interpretation of lay experience is from Yves Congar whose *Lay People in the Church* was the most definitive treatment of the laity by a Roman Catholic theologian before Vatican II, as noted in the introduction. For that reason and also because of its intrinsic merit, an essay by Congar which appeared in 1972 serves as a good starting point to review the key theological interpretations of the laity after Vatican II. "My Pathfindings in the Theology of Laity and Ministries" is a sort of revisionist look at *Lay People* in light of what had transpired since that book was written.

Congar affirms again his attempt to define lay persons in positive terms, which he had done in *Lay People* by stressing their secularity and by showing the particular way lay persons share in the threefold office of Christ. These points Congar retains. However, he now sees that he defined priesthood and church office apart from their proper context, the community of faith.

In characteristic humility, Congar judges his initial approach to be too linear: moving from Jesus to the apostles to the hierarchy to the faithful. In place of that sequence he would now prefer to stress the total community of the faithful as the abiding context and appropriate starting point for discussing the laity (and clergy as well). Community grounds every other distinction worth making. Moreover, the term which Congar favors to describe the laity's activity is ministries. Both the term and its plural form are significant.

As a synonym for ministries, Congar refers to "modes of service," which include a wide range of activities. All these works inhere in the community's calling; they help define what the community is to be and do. Congar welcomes and affirms a diversity and increase of services as long as they are part of the encompassing reality of community.

In revising his position in this way, Congar touches upon one of the consistent themes in the post-Vatican II literature on the laity: the faith community. When the faith community is the context for discussion, emphasis tends to be placed upon sacramental initiation rather than ordination, upon charism rather than office, upon service rather than structure. These shifts of emphasis are primarily aimed at clarifying and affirming who the laity are, but they are also helpful in clarifying and affirming who the clergy are. The more specific nature and role of the ordained and vowed members of the church are seen in their integral and holistic context, which is the faith community.

*Leonard Doohan*[8]

The second representative contribution comes from Leonard Doohan, a lay theologian who teaches at Spokane University. Writing in the journal, *Communio*, Doohan identifies six theological interpretations of the laity.

The first sees the laity as an "instrumental ministry." In this sense, the laity are instruments of the hierarchy, extensions of the church which functions under the authority of the ordained. Without denying the benefits of such an approach in the past, Doohan is convinced the theological and cultural shifts since Vatican II make this approach obsolete, although it is still found in the attitudes and behavior of many clergy and some laity. The fundamental shift in ecclesiology which moves from a hierarchy-centered approach to a People of God community approach undercuts the instrumental notion. In addition, the increase in education, skills, expertise, and social position among the laity calls for something more than an instrumental role in the clergy's work.

The second theology understands the laity to be "an ecclesial presence to the world." This is a softening of the instrumental approach, but it retains the implicit dualism between church and world. It assumes that the world is unecclesial until and unless the laity bring to the world the ecclesial presence which they represent. Admittedly, this theology does affirm the ecclesial character of the laity, but it suggests that this ecclesial character is obtained from the church and brought to the world. There is not a corresponding appreciation for the divine presence already in the world, for any original grace events outside the aegis of the church, for the historical insertion of the divine life into the world by the laity over the centuries.

The third theological approach overcomes the deficien-

cies of the second approach by stressing "the world transforming character and mission of the laity." In this view,
the ecclesial, ministerial quality of lay activity is assumed
and the focus is on exercising it in the world. Specifically,
action for social justice, political reform, structural change
are the characteristic approaches of laity understood in this
way. The theological grounding for this view is the incarnation, according to which the divine life is shared in and
with the world. It is not channeled simply or exclusively
through the formal agency of the church. When pushed to
an extreme, this approach could dangerously reduce the
transcendent dimension of the divine life and suggest that
human effort alone can achieve the goals of the Kingdom
of God.

If the same energy were directed not at the world but at
"reforming and restructuring the church," Doohan's
fourth model would appear. The church in this view is seen
not in isolation from the world but as a model for the
world. Efforts to make the church everything that it can
and should be are undertaken with an eye on the impact
such witness will have for the world. The way the church
works out its human conflicts, how it balances individual
and communal concerns, what value it places on pluralism,
etc., are all contributions to a world struggling with the
same issues. This approach presupposes a high level of
commitment to the church and to improving its structures
and styles of operation. It also leaves open the question
whether this restructuring will really work within the
church and whether it will have much impact on the world
outside the church.

A fifth theology of the laity is "heuristic." This approach is guided by the biblical image of the pilgrimage.
According to this image the church and the world are seen

in process. Structures and symbols of unity are less important than commitment, experiment, intense community experience, and a trusting openness to the work of God in
our lives. This approach advocates a high level of personal
identification and may weaken other forms of belonging to
the church. It also tends to undercut the informative and
normative value of tradition which could result in isolation
of the present from the past.

The final approach to a theology of the laity is an echo
of what Yves Congar had advocated—"a total ecclesiology." Such an ecclesiology would provide a holistic context, but it is not clear what a total ecclesiology is. Because
there are various ecclesiologies operative today, theologians prefer to speak of models of church rather than a
single, inclusive ecclesiology. It is important to recognize,
with Vatican II, that ecclesiology or faith community is the
proper context for discussing any roles in the church. But
that only begins the discussion.

Doohan's survey captures most of the theological approaches put forward since Vatican II. It is a helpful over-
view, enlarging on Congar's own reflections and gathering
the thoughts of other authors. These reflections by individual theologians, clergy and lay, are complemented by
reflections from groups, also clergy and lay.

## Chicago Declaration of Christian Concern[9]

The third representative interpretation comes from a
group of laity and clergy who are members of the Chicago
Catholic Community. Their Declaration was issued in
December 1977 and was a critical assessment of the trend
in lay activity as the signers of the Declaration perceived it.
An immediate and widespread reaction was generated by
the Declaration prompting the formation of a National

Center for the Laity, publication of a newsletter, and the sponsorship of a National Assembly of the Laity at Notre Dame University in March 1979.

The declaration begins with the experience of the local church in Chicago and moves at once to a critical interpretation of what had been happening. "While many in the church exhaust their energies arguing internal issues, albeit important ones, such as the ordination of women and a married clergy, the laity who spend most of their time and energy in the professional and occupational world appear to have been deserted." In a series of rhetorical questions and laments, the signers urge a return to the vision of Vatican II.

That vision identifies hope for social justice and world peace with the church's saving mission and embraces all the institutions of society as well as individuals. This hard-won affirmation is in danger of being lost by an emphasis on internal church matters which leads to a devaluation of the unique ministry of lay men and women. Such a tendency is reinforced by the single-handed efforts of many priests to change social structures and public policies from the outside, giving a double mistaken impression: that priests are the primary ones to do this and that it is best done from outside the very systems which are to be changed.

Partly as a result of the direction many priests have taken, a dangerous gap has developed with organizations and networks of lay persons to accomplish these same goals precisely where lay people live and work. The admitted incorporation of social justice concerns into the bureaucracy of the church is no substitute for such designated organizations. Neither is a capitulation of the gospel to various secular ideologies and strategies for change that usurp the gospel as if it endorsed the specific plan or program advocated by the ideology.

The entire declaration is a pointed critique and challenge to affirm the ecclesial nature of lay activity in the world (Doohan's third model). The Declaration states unequivocally that "the church is as present to the world in the ordinary roles of lay Christians as it is in the ecclesiastical roles of bishop and priest, though the styles of each differ." No clerical extension is needed for the church to be present through the laity.

At the same time the laity are challenged to reexamine their participation in internal church activities (Doohan's fourth model). Nowhere are these categorically opposed by the declaration, but the tendency to focus energy in this way is seen as a mistake and in need of correcting.

In some ways the Chicago declaration echoes the thrust of Catholic Action. It clearly identifies the primary role of the laity in the world and the primary role of the clergy in the church. Moreover, the clergy are expected to provide the programs and motivation for lay activity in the world. All this is put in a Vatican II context but the underlying orientation is very traditional.

The Declaration struck a resounding chord and focused one of the key issues in the postconciliar church: the tension between serving in the church and serving in the world.

### Called and Gifted[10]

The final representative reflection on the laity comes from the U.S. Catholic bishops. In November 1980 they issued a statement commemorating the fifteenth anniversary of the Vatican II Declaration on the Lay Apostolate. As the bishops make clear in their introduction to this brief reflection, their intention is to "praise the Lord for what is happening among the laity and proclaim as well as we can what we have been experiencing and learning from them."

This tone of openness and positive concern imbues the document. The bishops' reflections are set in the context of the church as the People of God. This image immediately establishes a connection with Vatican II and provides a comprehensive category for discussing the laity. The role of the laity within the People of God is described in terms of a call—a call essentially and initially from God but uttered recently through the church at Vatican II. It is clear that the laity have already heard this call and are responding to it. The bishops want only to reinforce this and to celebrate what has been happening in order to intensify the role of the laity in the future. Their observations are presented as the call to adulthood, holiness, ministry, and community.

### 1. *Adulthood*

This opening point is a key to the entire statement. The bishops' fundamental affirmation of the laity is that they are adults. This means first of all that they are adults in the faith, but of course religious and psychological maturity go together. Therefore, adult believers will be more independent and self-directive than immature believers. The bishops advocate this and acknowledge that "the experience of lay persons 'as church members' has not always reflected this understanding of adulthood."

The stress of the bishops on the adulthood of the laity is consistent with the American concern for personal growth and development of the individual. This tendency has already had a major impact on American pastoral care and catechetics, especially in the area of adult education. The bishops want to build on the positive elements of these developments.

A further implication of the stress on adulthood is that the proper form of clergy-laity relations is one of shared responsibility. In shared responsibility there is less insistence on the privileges of office and more attention to the quality of interaction and the combining of talents for the mission of the church. A spirit of interdependence should emerge and with it a new respect for each one's talents, dedication, and gifts.

### 2. *Holiness*

The second call which the bishops discuss is the call to holiness. Here too they follow Vatican II and speak of the universal call to holiness which is heard and responded to in a special way by the laity. "Not only are lay people included in God's call to holiness, but theirs is a unique call requiring a unique response which itself is a gift of the Holy Spirit."

The bishops want to encourage the laity to cultivate their own spirituality for the good of the whole church. "It is characteristic that lay men and women hear the call to holiness in the very web of their existence." This is in contrast to expecting the laity to conform to a spirituality developed for religious or monastic communities or even diocesan clergy. In this regard the adulthood of the laity is again implied, for no one else can tell the laity what their own distinctive spirituality should be. It is for them to discover.

### 3. *Ministry*

In the third call the bishops stress the participation of all the baptized "in some form of ministry." In describing the ministry of the laity the bishops cite first ministry in the world. In doing so they want to underline the importance of this work for which the laity are uniquely positioned. More than that, the bishops recognize that the contemporary world presents challenges which are unprecedented. The laity must face them, not alone to be sure, but creatively, as believing adults.

Not to be forgotten, of course, is the ministry of lay persons in the church. In a special way the bishops mention the many volunteers who have served and continue to serve the church. The new ministries opening up for professionally trained lay persons are also affirmed along with the practical problems entailed such as insufficient jobs for those qualified, low salaries, lack of benefits. Much more briefly do the bishops mention the role of women and advocate an increased role "to the extent possible."

### 4. *Community*

The final call, to community, is made against the background of numerous small, independent Christian communities. The bishops stress the role of the family as a model for church community but do not go further in recognizing the diversity of family situations which exist today. Even the problems that are mentioned are in reference to the basic, nuclear family.

It does seem clear that ministry to families is a major priority among lay people. Exactly what that ministry should consist of and how it should be carried out are open questions.

At the conclusion of their statement the bishops indicate that they have tried to offer their perceptions and have spoken in order to listen. The things they have been hearing raise the key issues which a contemporary theological interpretation of the lay experience should address. There are four such issues.

## VALUE OF MINISTRY IN THE WORLD

The key question here is: Will ministry in the world be considered just as important as ministry in the church? This, at any rate, is the question for lay persons in societal activity and for many of those engaged in independent activity. For others, the question is less weighted: How does ministry in the world *relate to* ministry in the church? This is how the question is felt by those in voluntary and church professional activity. Dutiful Catholics may not see this as much of an issue, except insofar as official church teaching advocates social responsibility as part of what it means to be a good Catholic.

Although the role of the laity in the world has traditionally been cited as their special arena for action, the impression remains that real ministry is done in the church, especially by the ordained. The emergence of church professional lay ministers may help to reinforce this idea. If their work is seen as the model for lay ministry, then the manifold acts of service performed in society by countless women and men apart from church auspices will appear to be less than ministry, and perhaps of less value. If this idea prevailed, it could weaken the religious commitment to improve the world by the very people who are in the best position to do so (as the Chicago Declaration warned).

A theological interpretation of the lay experience has to face this question of the value of ministry in the world and its relation to ministry in the church. A second question is closely related to this—the role of the clergy.

*Role of the Clergy*

The key question here is: Are the clergy able to interact without fear and defensiveness with laity who engage in church professional, societal, or independent activity? Can they recognize and encourage the charisms of lay persons who do voluntary or dutiful work? And can they let their own gifts be challenged and shaped by the laity?

These are the more pointed concerns hidden in the general and less threatening discussions of shared responsibility, enablement, mutual ministry, coordination of services, etc. If these terms mean in practice that laity are asked to share in the clergy's work and more or less on the clergy's terms (or without any clergy support or involvement), then not much has changed. Laity and lay activity will still be defined essentially in relation to clergy and ordained activity, which means they will be defined negatively—as non-ordained, unable to do all the ordained can do, secondary to the primacy of the ordained ministers. This is the attitude that most lay people resist (except perhaps the dutiful).

To focus these questions on the clergy is not to overlook the fact that the same questions must be asked of the laity. Indeed, there are many clergy who see the laity as equals and try to involve them in church ministry or support their societal work but meet only indifference or resistance (especially from the dutiful again). It is clearly not a one-way street. Nonetheless, a greater burden rests with the clergy, given the dominant emphasis of the past on their role.

A theological interpretation of the lay experience has to be sensitive to this situation and try to find suitable ways of expressing the real differences and varied relationships among all the People of God.

### Role of Spirituality

The third issue is spirituality. Lay persons in all five types of activity seek spiritual nourishment, although they have different expectations. In general, liturgy and Scripture are essential elements. How these resources are connected to the daily experience of lay persons is the key question. The search for integration is usually more acute among laity engaged in church professional, societal, and independent activity. Those who volunteer and are dutiful evidence more ease with leaving their ordinary life experience and entering a different kind of experience in church.

From the point of view of spirituality, of course, prayer and faith should permeate one's whole life, without forcing one to abandon or devalue the experiences which constitute that life. Dualism is not desirable in the spiritual life. On the other hand, spiritual growth does involve change, insight, deliberate attention to life experience. It is not automatic and it is rarely solitary. Thus, the quest for lay spirituality leads to the fourth area—community.

A theological interpretation of the lay experience should open up some possibilities for the spiritual life that integrate Scripture and liturgy with the lay experience without abandoning that experience or extolling it in an unreflective way.

### Role of Community

The key question here is: What makes the ordinary groupings of lay persons a Christian community? Or is community an experience, once again, that requires people to leave their customary situations? These questions parallel the other three and are felt most keenly by laity in the church professional and independent areas. Voluntary and dutiful lay persons tend to be satisfied with the level of community they experience at church; societal lay persons often desire a deeper experience of community but their priorities in society claim the time and energy it would take to foster it.

Community should not be artificial nor should it compete with other important groupings in a person's life. The goal is to find ways to integrate explicit Christian community experiences with other experiences (not necessarily Christian or explicitly religious) in a person's life.

A theological interpretation of the lay experience should offer some suggestions for doing this and may even serve as a reason for people to come together and experience themselves as community while they reflect theologically on their lives.

These four issues constitute a challenge to the whole church. They are not exclusively lay issues, although they are experienced by lay persons in a particular way. Theology has a limited contribution to make, and the reflections offered in the next chapters are only one suggestion. But it is one that tries to be faithful to the experience of lay people today and to incorporate the four central issues which have emerged from that experience.

# CHAPTER TWO

## *The Dominant Factor: Lay Ministry*[1]

AFTER gathering the experience of the laity, it is important to identify the dominant factor in that experience. As used here, a dominant factor is one that gives unity to everything else which makes up the total experience. In providing such unity, the dominant factor invests the elements of an experience with its own character. With regard to the experience of the laity since Vatican II, the dominant factor seems to be ministry.

This term has become the standard way of referring to the activity of lay people today although lay persons do not necessarily think of themselves as ministers or describe their activity as ministry. John Coleman in his essay, "The Future of Ministry," observes both the rapid establishment of this term to describe the lay role and also the fact that it has taken hold with virtually no public debate or official agreement. From a sociological and theological point of view such an event is indeed noteworthy, for it signals that contemporary lay activity has a dynamic, self-defining quality. Unlike classic Catholic Action, lay ministry appears to be a rather independent phenomenon.

Of course, the definition and use of a term like ministry is of interest to many people, not least the episcopal hierarchy. In fact, several national conferences of bishops have tried to clarify the use of the term ministry and related concepts like service, gifts, office. Their efforts have been paralleled by those of theologians and canon lawyers, all of whom have produced a sizable literature so far.

In general these discussions deal with what activities should be called ministry (the scope of the term), how ministries relate to other activities, how persons should be prepared to exercise their ministry, and what sort of recognition or authorization is needed to do ministry. These topics will frame the first part of this chapter.

## Scope of the Term[2]

Much of the theological discussion has focused on the scope of the term ministry. Those who take their lead from Vatican II usage restrict the use of the term to the work of the ordained (deacon, priest, bishop) or officially installed minister (lector, acolyte). This restriction is not meant to minimize the value of what others contribute by their activity but to specify how the term should be used so it will have a definite meaning. The argument is that if everything which Christians do is called ministry, then the term itself will lose any specific meaning.

In fact, the term has been used in a more restricted sense in the past, which is why the acceptance of a broader meaning now is so remarkable. One of the most helpful descriptions which combines both the traditional and contemporary emphases is that of the Asian bishops. They use ministry to refer to those functions which pertain to the essential activity of the church. For this reason they are stable (if not permanent) elements in the makeup of church and those who exercise them are presumed to have a stable (if not permanent) commitment to do just these tasks. Other good works are referred to as services. These are important to the life of the church but are not essential to its very existence. Both ministries and services are grounded in the gifts which the Spirit bestows on individuals. In this schema ministry is virtually equated with offices in the church and with the corresponding responsibilities to perform the functions which constitute the inner life of the church while other important activities are called services.

Helpful as this distinction is, not everyone shares it —especially those who are not located in the official structure of the church but still consider their service to be ministry. These people use the term to describe the exercise of the gifts which they are given by the Holy Spirit for the good of others. Among these gifts are certainly the offices just mentioned, but ministry has a wider scope than that. The term is defined, not so much in relation to the structure of the church or even the essential functions which constitute the church, but rather in relation to the gifts of the Spirit and the needs of the community.

It seems clear that the key words are community, gift (charism), service, ministry. How these words are defined and related is an open question. No attempt to settle the discussion once and for all will or can succeed. Indeed, the very attempt to do so can introduce an unwelcome feeling that someone is trying to control what is ultimately uncontrollable.

On the other hand, the discussion has some indirect advantages. It focuses attention on all that *is* going on among the People of God, and it raises the importance of determining how all this activity can best interrelate. Because of the preponderance of the clergy in the past, there is a tendency to view the emergence of new ministries from the perspective of ordained ministry and to relate lay ministry to the traditional work of the clergy. In this case, ordination is the model of ministry and other activities are interpreted in relation to it.

There are alternative approaches which begin with a more inclusive category than ordination. Undoubtedly the most frequently cited starting point of this kind is Christian initiation. This does have a certain equalizing and unifying appeal insofar as all other distinctions in ministry presuppose baptism. However, Christian initiation is not a univocal event always the same for all people. Initiation is a process. From this it follows that one may be more-or-less initiated relative to everyone else. No one, of course, knows what the degrees of difference are, but if certain members (the clergy, the vowed members of religious communities) are assumed to be more initiated, as symbolized by the special character of ordination, then a subtle but important difference between clergy and laity is reintroduced which affects the unifying potential of initiation.

A mere definition of terms will not answer the practical questions, but a perceptive interpretation of what is going on can provide a practical framework for doing so. Ministry is the term that stimulates this kind of inquiry. It has become the dominant theological factor in interpreting the experience of the laity.

### Relationships[3]

The thoroughgoing renewal of Vatican II set in motion a great number of changes in the church. These changes gave rise to a variety of starting points, emphases, and goals which have coexisted, and sometimes conflicted with one another, in the postconciliar church. The diverse activity and different points of view (represented by the five categories of lay activity described in chapter one) call for a new order, a way of interpreting the living church that respects and enhances the diversity rather than fears and curtails it. Ministry is a test case and a helpful contribution to this concern for order in the postconciliar church.

It is very difficult to spell out the relationships between

ministry and other activities in a way that exemplifies a healthy order. The gifts of the Spirit seem to be a viable starting point for interrelating ministry and other services. In this context all services derive from the gifts of the Spirit. But if some gifts are considered more essential or more important than others, then the same division creeps back in. This sometimes occurs when the traditional claim of an essential difference between the ordained priesthood and the priesthood of the baptized is made. When an essential difference is introduced into an otherwise homogeneous view of ministry, those who feel themselves to be different only in degree or function are alienated.

This has led some to emphasize community as the proper starting point for a discussion of ministry. This does provide a larger context, but the question is whether community itself is defined widely enough. If it is taken to refer in the first place to organized church community, then the organizers (clergy) become the focus. And there is a tendency to concentrate activity within that organized community, usually in terms of building community. If this happens, the same pattern and problems arise as with initiation or the gifts of the Spirit.

The problem of describing ministry from a starting point within the confines of church life suggests that a different approach is needed. If the church as a whole were seen in the larger context of its relation to the world, then ministerial relations within the church might be harmonized more easily. In other words, by taking the church's social mission as the entry point a more inclusive and valuable interpretation may result.

I shall develop this more fully in chapter four but a brief word here is in order. The most dynamic impetus for viewing the social mission of the church since Vatican II has come from liberation theology.

In this theology, liberation may be understood in a threefold sense. First, it is liberation in order to satisfy human survival needs: food, clothing, shelter, health care. It is a central value that persons be free to satisfy these needs for themselves rather than being kept artificially dependent on others. Liberation aims at creating the conditions in which this is possible, so this level of liberation is directed primarily toward socioeconomic and political change.

Second, there is liberation in order to affirm human dignity and human rights. Each person has an intrinsic dignity precisely as a human being. One way to affirm this dignity is to safeguard human rights. When these are violated, even unconsciously or indeliberately, liberation is required. This level of liberation is primarily directed to cultural and interpersonal values and practice.

Third, there is liberation from sin and death. This level of liberation is beyond the capacity of human persons to achieve by themselves. It requires a savior. Here Christianity makes its most distinctive claim that Jesus is that savior. But our liberation from sin and death by Jesus is not isolated from our continuing liberation for human dignity and for satisfying survival needs. Christian liberation is not reduced to these, but it may not exclude them either.

In this understanding, liberation is comprehensive; it includes all persons and all dimensions of human life, especially that dimension which humans alone are unable to overcome: sin and death. Liberation provides a context within which one may locate other, more specific ministerial functions like evangelizing, catechizing, sacramentalizing, community building. Liberation understood in this way offers both a theological perspective to view the various forms of exercising the church's mission and a criterion to evaluate how they interrelate. The implications of this perspective may be seen in regard to relations between laity and clergy, the scope of ministry, and relations between world and church.

### 1. *Laity-Clergy Relations*

From a liberation perspective the relationship between laity and clergy is one of mutual liberating. The guiding concern is not who is superior, who makes final decisions, who judges the acceptability of actions but rather how laity and clergy free each other so that together they may be a more liberating force in society. This view underscores the value of ministry in society, one of the central issues cited at the end of chapter one.

For example, the mature exercise of gifts by the laity in the areas of spirituality and community support can free the clergy from an exaggerated responsibility to *provide for* people the means of salvation as if people could not be saved any other way. This type of liberation leads to a stronger relationship than when the laity free the clergy from some of their tasks, e.g., in finances, religious education, or parish visitation. Something deeper and more unifying happens when the laity demonstrate their spiritual self-reliance.

On the other hand, if the clergy communicate their honest struggle to understand and live the Christian commitment (especially in society), this can free the laity to affirm their own questions, uncertainties, and disagreements with the Christian tradition (a need especially of societal or independent lay persons). It is more liberating to acknowledge and share doubts and confusion than to maintain a pretense of assurance, especially in regard to decisions about moral questions, beliefs about sin, suffering, evil, and retribution, assumptions about the unity of the faith or its interpretation. Liberation can provide a practical context which strengthens the relationship between laity and clergy by freeing the members to be more fully who they are.

### 2. Scope of Ministry

From a liberation perspective the definition of ministry is primarily qualitative. Ministry refers to those activities which have a liberating effect. Thus, volunteering to teach in the religious education program is ministry if the actual teaching/learning is liberating. Likewise, preaching is ministry if the hearers are freed to enter the eucharist and the world.

Since this liberating result cannot be predetermined, the definition of any act as ministry is to be found in its effects. Of course, a person may intend a specific act to be liberative, and to this degree the activity may be considered ministerial. But the final determination depends on what actually happens. Now, there are many good works which have neither the intention nor the effect of liberation. Such works are not valueless or undesirable; they simply do not fit the definition of ministry from a liberation perspective.

Viewed in this way liberation offers a criterion for affirming ministry whether it occurs through an office, charism, service, gift, commission, career, or any other specific form. This would not automatically unify all the forms of Christian activity, but it would provide a practical framework for relating them to one another. Since the liberative quality is based on the effect of the activity and not on the formal status of the one doing it, liberation would be a criterion applicable to all Christian activities from nurturing one's family, to planning a Holy Week liturgy, to making ethical business decisions, to teaching a class on liberation.

One of the implications of this approach is that the term ministry is not reserved exclusively for the work of certain persons (such as ordained or installed ministers). Whereas all initiated Christians are called to help in the mission of the church and some are called to fill specifically designated offices, those whose work has a liberating effect are considered ministers.

Another implication of this approach is that it puts great stress on each exercise of ministry, because ministry is determined by the effects in people's lives. There is nothing automatic or predetermined about ministry. This can also be interpreted as an overemphasis on functions and a lack of faith in God's role in acts of service. However, if the threefold level of liberation is kept in mind, then the qualitative, personal, and spiritual aspects are preserved in ministerial functioning while the focus stays with service rather than status.

## 3. *World-Church Relations*

From a liberation perspective the relation of the world and the church is one of mutual freeing. This parallels the laity-clergy relation but is more inclusive. Liberation is not an exclusively religious or theological term, especially in its first two meanings (human survival and human dignity) although these can be given a specific theological interpretation. At the same time, liberation does have a distinctive theological meaning regarding sin and death. Liberation sets up a mutual relation between world and church in which each has something distinctive to contribute to the other while both are affected by the same common concerns.

A liberation perspective can explain how "action on behalf of justice and participation in the transformation of the world" are "a constitutive dimension of the preaching of the Gospel," as the 1971 Synod of Bishops proclaimed. Any genuine liberative act is on the way toward total liberation from sin and death. A church characterized by liberation would be a model and stimulus for a world in need of liberation (as noted in Doohan's models of ecclesial presence to the world and world-transforming mission). At the same time, instances of worldly liberation would remind and challenge the church to its liberative mission. The laity, at least at the present time, hold a unique transitional position in this relationship precisely as liberating agents in both the church and the world.

## *Preparation-Recognition*[4]

No matter how ministry is defined, it lends itself to some type of preparation and continuing development. How formal and how programmatic this preparation should be depends partly on the nature of the ministry in question and partly on the nature of ministry.

Some ministries require more skill and training than others. Care of the sick or counseling or community organizing (especially in a liberating sense) require some degree of trained competence. Sometimes a person's ministry is an extension of services for which a person already has training or experience, e.g., group leadership, social services, health care, teaching, organizing, counseling. In this case, what may be needed is a ministerial identity more than basic skill development.

If the nature of ministry is defined in liberative terms, then preparation programs should be an experience of liberation for the participants (along the lines sketched in the previous section). This would require prime attention to be given to each individual and to *that* person's needs and possibilities for a freeing experience. The same is true if ministry is defined in some other way. In other words, any formal program should manifest and facilitate the nature of ministry as it is understood in that program.

Along with the question of how much and what kind of training, there is the question of who should provide it and where it should be located. If diocesan personnel provide it (as is the case in many lay training programs now in operation), the orientation tends to be rather general and probably determined by a diocesan perspective on the needs and functions of ministry. This is understandable but it could overlook some of the specific differences among parishes or other local settings for ministry.

To counteract this, some training programs are diocesan initiated and supported, but parish based. They aim at bringing the resources *to* people at the parish level and building programs around particular local needs. This is especially conducive to a liberative view of ministry. While this moves the training closer to the actual location of lay ministers, it carries with it administrative and logistical problems as well as a lack of adequate resources for each place or each local need.

No matter what the specific format or goal, the overriding aim of any training program for ministry is to help persons recognize and develop their gifts in a spiritual/faith environment. A key to achieving this is for each participant to experience being a community of faith with others who are preparing for ministry. There is a frequent complaint that this doesn't happen often enough. It can't happen at all unless it is intentionally included in the preparation program.

When spiritual development is integrated into ministry training programs the tendency to overprofessionalize the training can be better controlled. In addition, if the faith/spiritual development of lay persons is a central feature, then their life situations can also shape the program. Whether they are married, have families, are single, divorced, widowed, will make a difference in their own spirituality and in the possibilities for experiencing faith community.

Part of the preparation for ministry is the need to recognize those who do it. The issue of recognition cuts both ways. On the one hand, it expresses the status of lay activity as ministry. On the other hand, it too easily suggests a dependence on ordained ministry if recognition comes from the hierarchy. This in turn can lead to a reclericalizing of ministry and the assumption that hierarchical control or approval is needed for lay activity to be authentic.

From a liberation perspective recognition should be given by those who have been liberated by a person's ministry. Since this liberating can only occur *as a result* of ministry, recognition should be given at intervals after a preparation program has been completed, or at least after a person has begun to act with the skills and experience acquired in a preparation program.

## Meaning of Lay Ministry

These practical and programmatic decisions are being worked out by thousands of dedicated persons throughout the U.S. Their experience is an indispensible testing ground for future development. The advancement that results from "doing" training programs is complemented by the quest for a clearer perception of what such programs are preparing people to do, i.e., what is lay ministry? As already indicated in this chapter, that question elicits several different definitions.

But the ultimate significance of the term lay ministry is not to be found in a definition, because the real thrust of the term is toward an experience, a feeling, a sensed meaning. This is what the phrase lay ministry seems to express. The task is not so much to define the term as to interpret it, to describe that elusive reality that it points to. As I have been exposed to the term and listened to people use it, I have detected three strands of meaning. These three strands form an overlapping cluster that yields a certain coherence and unity (as a dominant factor should) to the rest of the field of lay experience. The other experiences in that field inherit their character from the meaning of lay ministry.

1. *From Importance to Authenticity*

The first strand of meaning stretches from the feeling of importance to the feeling of authenticity. The word ministry suggests an importance which other words like apostolate, good works, and service do not. This sense of importance comes, no doubt, from the association of the word ministry with the ministerial priesthood of holy orders and the minor ministries of church office.

At the same time the word ministry does not necessarily imply the idea of church office or the sacrament of orders. It is free of those formal positions, but it retains the feeling of importance which they convey. Ministry points *toward* that kind of service (ordained) without *being* that kind of service. The dissimilarity is as crucial as the similarity, because lay ministry is not an adjunct or extension of ordained ministry, although like ordained ministry it is important.

Another source of influence on the meaning of the term comes from the ecumenical field. Contact with Protestant churches especially has had a positive impact on Catholic laity. The quite familiar use of ministry in other Christian traditions to describe the role of church members is easily transferable to Roman Catholicism. This does not explain everything, of course, but it opens up an additional source of experience for shaping the future development of lay ministry in the Roman Catholic church.

Ordinarily, lay persons who respond to the Spirit's gifts in their lives do so in a church which is dominated by the clergy. Hence, a new development like lay ministry must claim its importance in relation to the existing ministry of the ordained.

To do so, lay ministers become assertive in order to get others to notice who they are and what they do. Sometimes this assertiveness can become belligerent, and a basic desire for recognition can turn into competition for attention and influence. Even if this occurs, it should be seen for what it is—a desire to be taken seriously. At this point on the spectrum, however, the desire is still focused on the acceptance and evaluation of others.

As lay ministers appropriate and exercise their gifts it becomes less important that others acknowledge their ministry. The intrinsic satisfaction of knowing that one is gifted and empowered by the Holy Spirit for liberative action is ample reinforcement and authentication. Of course, no one reaches such a level alone or all at once. Affirmation and support and feedback from others help to insure that one's actions *are* prompted by the Spirit and do liberate according to God's purpose.

At this end of the continuum more energy can be spent exercising one's ministry and less energy spent securing recognition of one's ministry from others. People will be found all along the spectrum from importance to authenticity. The word ministry is elastic enough to cover this full range of feeling which is associated with the experience of lay ministry.

The ultimate basis for this whole continuum is, of course, the Holy Spirit. It is the Spirit who establishes both the importance and the authenticity of ministerial gifts. Other persons may acknowledge, reinforce, encourage, facilitate, and celebrate the importance of lay ministry, but only the Spirit initiates it and guides it from importance to authenticity.

## 2. *From Equality to Complementarity*

As commonly used today, the term ministry covers a wide range of specific activities. Without distinguishing them further, the word ministry imparts a certain fundamental equality to all the different functions it encompasses. This sense of equality is similar to the previous note of importance. Lay ministry is both important and equal. Equal at least in the sense of having an equal claim to be exercised, of being divinely inspired, of being no less ministerial than ordained ministry even if the activities themselves are less time consuming or central to the stability of the faith community as a whole.

The feeling of equality, like the feeling of importance, is somewhat competitive. But it moves toward complementarity as persons feel less need to argue for the equality of their ministry and more desire to enhance the effect of their ministry. Effect is enhanced when specific activities are carried out as part of a pattern of ministries which complement one another. Complementarity calls for the ability and maturity to focus attention on ministry as an interlocking, dynamic exercise of God's gifts rather than on one's own particular, limited contribution.

Once again, it is unlikely that a person can come to this stance alone or quickly. But when persons are received and treated as equals in the ministry, they can leave behind the need to assert their equality and move toward the more creative and satisfying project of blending their ministry with that of others.

The ultimate basis for this strand of experience within lay ministry is the vision of God for the world as it takes shape through the lives and decisions of women and men in history. God's vision of how the many can work together to become one is imparted to all the faithful. And the energy to move from a concern for equality to an exercise of complementarity is powered by the vision of God which always takes seriously what happens through each person's ministry.

### 3. *From Ownership to Stewardship*

The ministerial gifts each person receives are truly given to the recipient. They become part of the person. They are not separable from who the person is but help constitute and define who the person is. When a person recognizes and affirms this, it is ownership.

Ownership of one's gifts implies self-possession and gives rise to the desire to assert oneself *as* a minister (even if the word is not used). Enacting what is owned (one's ministry) can be especially difficult if it means initiating new roles or changing existing patterns of ministry. There can also be personal conflict if others resist one's ministry. When this happens, lay ministers may perceive the resistance as directed, not just at their ministry, but at themselves as ministers. When persons really own their ministry, their activity can never be simply a function; it is an expression of who they are. For this reason, they cannot allow themselves to be controlled by the judgments of others. Ownership means they must minister because the impetus and empowerment for it has come from God.

But ownership does not mean private possession. It is not enough to have one's ministry; one must also exercise it. All ministry is ultimately for others (for their liberation). The condition of others gives the actual shape to the exercise of ministry. This leads from ownership to stewardship. Stewardship means the responsible care of what one owns so that others may benefit. The connection is very intimate. In fact, responding to others often enables people to recognize what they own and to claim the gifts given to them by the Spirit as their own. This sense of ownership-stewardship brings with it a feeling of authority that prompts a person to act, to take initiative, to respond creatively, to generate ministerial service when the situation calls for it.

The ultimate basis for this strand of meaning is community, but community as the experience of persons coming together in response to one another to manifest concretely their response to the Lord. This gives a more functional character to community than is usually done, and it stresses the occasions of stewardship rather than the structures or procedures for it.

To sum up, lay ministry is the dominant theological factor in the experience of the laity since Vatican II. Lay ministry refers, not so much to a precisely defined activity, but to an experience, a feeling for what it means to be a lay person after Vatican II. The experiential meaning of lay ministry encompasses several overlapping and interconnecting feelings described here as ranging from importance to authenticity, from equality to complementarity, from ownership to stewardship.

Lay ministry is dominant but not exclusive. There are other, contrasting factors which situate lay ministry and give it added impact. Two of these contrasts will be discussed in the next chapter: laity-clergy relations and world-church relations.

# CHAPTER THREE

## *The Contrasting Factors*

THE last chapter discussed lay ministry as the dominant theological factor in the experience of the laity since Vatican II. A dominant factor appears as dominant only in relation to contrasting factors. The contrasts are usually found within the same general field of experience as the dominating factor. Contrasts function in the same way as background does for foreground in painting or subthemes do for themes in music or drama. Contrast intensifies feeling and broadens the import of the dominant factor.

With regard to the experience of lay ministry two contrasting factors are evident: the relationship between laity and clergy and the relationship between world and church. These are also two of the key themes from chapter one and are the focus of the rest of this chapter.

### *Laity-Clergy Relations*[1]

It is almost impossible to disengage the experience of lay ministry from the contrasting and more inclusive relationship of laity and clergy. The contrast generates a mixture of positive and negative feelings. The mixture is fairly even. At the present time, the laity as a whole seem to have neither unqualified admiration and enthusiasm for the clergy nor overt, widespread feelings of anticlericalism. There is often frustration, disappointment, yearning for something better, but also appreciation, patience, understanding of the role of the clergy and the difficulties they face in fulfilling it.

In general, the laity-clergy contrast may be analyzed in

three important areas: history, theology, and current practice. Each area contributes something to the overall experience and interpretation of lay ministry.

### 1. *History*[2]

In its broadest strokes the history of laity-clergy relations shows a movement from equality (biblical times), to separation (Constantinian era), to subordination (medieval age), to support (after the Reformation), to initiation (after Vatican II). The actual history is more complicated than that, of course, and cannot be comprehensively reproduced here. But a few highlights will help to clarify how this history influences the current experience of lay ministry.

At the outset of the Christian movement a fundamental equality seemed to be felt among the followers of Jesus. There were certain obvious differences, of course. Eyewitnesses of Jesus had some distinction relative to those who only heard of Jesus. The Twelve had a special role in the first communities. Widows were viewed in a special way. And there were the inevitable, powerful personalities like Peter and Paul and the Beloved Disciple.

But the prevailing conviction among Christians seemed to be what was expressed in 1 Peter 2:9-10. The followers of Jesus saw themselves as the new People of God. Whatever else differentiated them, they were all equally incorporated into Christ. That was *their* "dominant experience." It served as the basis for appeals to unity and the correction of moral and ritual deviations.

No doubt this mentality was aided by the condition of Judaism at the time of Jesus. With no Temple, the priestly class was reduced in practice to equality with the rest of the People. In addition, the acceptance of Jesus by so many

Gentiles led to the decision that Judaism was not a necessary condition for being Christian. There were no privileged conditions or advantages that enhanced one's union with Jesus. Christianity gave Jew and Gentile a new (and equal) status vis-à-vis God and one another.

How consistently this equality was communicated and lived out is hard to say, in large part because there is so little evidence concerning those first generations of Christians. Perhaps the solidification of the role of the bishop, the veneration of the martyr, the practical influence of the apologist and catechist, the unique sanctity of the widow, the public witness of the penitent, the designated service of the deacon resulted, in practice, in the creation of distinctions that weakened the proclaimed equality of all the initiated.

Whatever the case in the first three hundred years, there is little question that the dawning of the Constantinian church (in the fourth century) brought with it a new experience of lay-clergy relations. That experience may be described as a separation. The focal point of Christian life began to shift from communities of believers within a city or region which was predominantly not Christian (and sometimes anti-Christian) to the city or region *as* the community of believers. A significant structural or organizational shift occurred simultaneously in which the primary identification of the church was separated from the people as such and was located with the leaders and office holders of the people.

As part of this separation, new roles emerged which had to do mostly with administration at a regional level. The specialized skills needed for these roles were "clerical" and were not possessed by the majority of people. The specification of clerical roles did not have to result in a separation among the people. But the church came to be identified more and more with the work of these clerics and the leaders they served, the bishops.

A counter movement developed in opposition to this clericalizing of the church. It was the monastic movement. Although intended to oppose the separatist impact of the clergy, the monasteries took a form of alternative separation, becoming enclaves within a village or region. In the antagonism between clergy and monks, the majority of the faithful were left in the lurch. Unskilled to be clerics, unable or unwilling to be monks, they were left with no very valued role.

Accompanying this twin separation was a subtle but real sense of subordination—or superiority, depending on which side of the laity-clergy relation one stands. A full-fledged attitude of superiority would, of course, be the antithesis of the original feeling of equality among believers. Such an antithesis appeared unmistakably in the medieval period (800-1500). Following the invasion of nomadic tribes into western Europe, the task of reconstructing society was taken up by rulers and educators and merchants who exercised real control over the masses. Even if the contests among the power holders were matches among relative equals, they were also matches among the elites. The majority of people were disregarded, considered inferior and subservient.

There were symbols of resistance to this, of course. Death was seen in popular piety as the great equalizer (instead of baptism). Festivals allowed for the reversal of roles and inversion of respect between the fool and the lord.

But the decisive reversal of the subordination of the laity came through Martin Luther. Seeing the extremes to which an unchecked superiority attitude had taken the hierarchy of his day, Luther sided with the people, affirming them as the chosen portion of God's election (even though Luther was not perfectly consistent in carrying out his basic affirmation).

The subsequent history of the laity in the Protestant tradition is a complex and valuable story. It displays a full range of theological and practical possibilities for lay-clergy relations. But the interest here is to stay with the history of the laity within Roman Catholicism.

In the post-Reformation era the subordination tendency remained strong in Roman Catholicism, but eventually began to be modified by a supportive attitude. The support was defined in terms of what the laity could give the clergy to help them do their job. The clergy's job remained primary, superior, all-important. The laity's support of the clergy was primarily threefold: monetary, spiritual, and attitudinal.

Material support included support of the clergy individually and of the church collectively. In the post-Reformation church this meant building churches, schools, seminaries, convents, orphanages, hospitals, monasteries, etc. The way laity could contribute to the defense of the true faith and the spread of the true church was to underwrite its cost and supply its material. This the laity did to a remarkable degree, right up to the present.

The laity offered spiritual support to the clergy, not only by prayer, but also by the religious formation of their families, which included the encouragement (sometimes arrangement) for one or more children to join the ranks of the clergy.

Perhaps the most pervasive form of laity support was attitudinal. And the dominant attitude was obedience. As Pius X said, quoted in the introduction, the multitude's duty is to let itself be led by its directors. At the height of polemics with Protestants and during the subsequent secular attacks from society, this attitude was a realistic survival strategy. Its effectiveness in meeting attacks was undeniable. The hindsight of history suggests, however, that such an obediential attitude was perpetuated long after it was strictly necessary. In fact, the supportive role of the laity began to emerge from passivity only in the mid-twentieth century.

The most explicit appeal for a supportive but more active laity was issued by Pius XI in the name of Catholic Action. As described in the introduction, Catholic Action was understood as the participation of the laity in the apostolate of the hierarchy. This approach maintained the superior position of the clergy while the supportive role of the laity continued their post-Reformation status. But Catholic Action intended that the laity would be more active than simply "doing what they were told." They were expected to move into areas of modern social life where the clergy were unable or unwilling to go. In those areas, at least, the laity were seen more as an extension than a support to the clergy.

With the stimulus of Catholic Action and the condition of Western society after World War II, the laity began to move into a new phase of relationship with the clergy. They began to initiate their own activity and service. This was especially evident in the U.S. After a strong period of lay initiative in the nineteenth century, the early twentieth century saw a restriction of lay activity. But beginning in the 1950s lay organizations began playing a larger role in church and society.

The advent of Vatican II gave this phase of lay initiative new impetus and importance. It is an emerging strand of experience which is surrounded by the still dominant history of separation-subordination-support. That historical backlog is not negligible. It tends to shape the overall environment in which a new experience struggles for space. The new experience of lay ministry is in contrast with the inherited pattern of lay-clergy relations. Knowing that pattern and understanding *its* origins helps to clarify how the contrast can be intensifying and broadening for lay ministry today. Of course, these historical developments were expressive of certain theological positions which also help to define the contrast.

## 2. *Theology*

The crucial theological issue in lay-clergy relations revolves around the claim that the ordained priesthood differs in essence, not merely degree, from the priesthood of all the faithful. The emergence of this understanding of an essential difference is part of the history just sketched and is difficult to disentangle from the early developments of Christian leadership and church organization.

Part of the problem is language; terms used today were either not used or were used differently in the past. Part of the problem is conceptual; the way people interpreted reality in the past made it easier to think about the church, the world, salvation in terms of essential differences and different kinds of reality (nature-grace, heaven-earth, matter-spirit). Today it is more customary to think in terms of differences of degree rather than of kind. Part of the problem is emotional; the feeling of reverence and respect for the clergy (reinforced by a celibate lifestyle and dedication to "spiritual" values) has created an experience of the clergy that feels quite different from that of ordinary Christians (and even from ordained Protestant ministers). This "otherness" has a powerful, symbolic value for many, laity and clergy alike, and operates as a kind of theology in practice, distinguishing and to some degree separating the ordained from the nonordained.

Insofar as the theological distinction creates a barrier between laity and clergy, it is a problem to be overcome. Currently, there are three basic approaches to resolve the theological problem of lay-clergy differences: historical-critical studies, alternative theoretical constructs, and symbolic declericalization.

## (a) *Historical-Critical Studies*[3]

The development of a theology of the ordained priesthood has been a topic of intense investigation for the last twenty-five years. Interest in this subject has been spurred by the general tendency to reexamine the historical origins of Christianity, a movement pioneered by biblical and liturgical scholars. Ecumenical interest has also encouraged a fresh look at the origins and development of one of the most divisive ecumenical issues: the pastoral/ministerial office. And some of the most important themes of Vatican II have fed into this effort and given additional impetus to the historical investigations: a People of God ecclesiology, the value of charisms, the desire for shared responsibility, the implications of baptism.

The most significant outcome of the historical-critical studies to date seems to be that the church has greater freedom to modify its structure of leadership (pastoral offices) than is ordinarily acknowledged. When theologians study the historical evidence, they find, instead of a single model or norm for all time, a principle of flexibility and adaptation that leaves decisions about the future shape of ministry dependent on future needs and circumstances.

This conclusion has direct bearing on such practical decisions as who shall preside at eucharist, who shall preach, who exercises authority in the name of and over communities of faith, what is the relation between the power of orders and the power of jurisdiction, how is ordination to be ritualized, who decides who shall be ordained, etc. Responsibilities and functions now reserved to the ordained could be more widely distributed among persons who are not ordained—if this interpretation of history is correct.

Historical-critical studies have not just opened up the possibility for sweeping change in the future; they have gleaned some basic criteria for enacting any such changes. Foremost among these criteria is the primacy of community. Community is primary in two senses: Any office or formal ministry should serve the community it belongs to and office holders should emerge from within the community. By and large in this context community refers to the local, parish community, or even smaller units of Christian gathering such as the ecclesial base communities in many parts of the world.

Historical-critical studies carefully trace the process by which key concepts (such as charism, priesthood, office, character, ordination) came into being, were clarified, and enacted. These studies are not necessarily systematic expositions of those concepts, even though they are often done by systematic theologians. There is another group of thinkers who approach the lay-clergy relationship as a theoretical issue and try to reconceptualize it, sometimes from theological and sometimes from other perspectives.

(b) *Alternative Theoretical Constructs*[4]
The theoretical approach to the theological problem of lay-clergy relations moves in two basic directions: theological alternatives and psycho-social alternatives. The first approach is to find a theological alternative to the notion of the sacramental character of ordination. In classic theology, the idea of sacramental character explains the

essential difference between the ordained priesthood and the baptized priesthood. Despite a nuanced interpretation of this view in classic theology, the popular understanding is to dichotomize conceptually what is unified experientially. Neither priest nor people really experience any essential difference because of ordination, and yet the church teaches that such a difference exists.

When the historical development of *this* concept is traced, it becomes clear that it is consistent with the general worldview and thought patterns of another age when dualisms and differences of essence were taken for granted. Ours is a different age; we tend to see reality in a more organic way. Differences of degree rather than of essence are usually assumed.

In order to communicate what ordination means, theological constructs generally take a larger, more inclusive category which ordination *exemplifies*. In this way it is distinctive as an example or model but remains intrinsically united to the more inclusive context and therefore an integral part of it rather than in a class (essence) by itself. The most common categories in this approach are community, charism, and mission—which were previously discussed as favored starting points for defining ministry in general.

Community is composed of those who have been initiated into Christ. At its core, initiation is into eucharistic community, and the eucharistic community as a whole is both agent and recipient of this gift. The designation of specific roles or offices within the community is to enact more easily or more fully both the agency and reception of eucharist. But in essence the ordained priesthood is an instance of the shared priesthood of the community and presupposes the community for its very existence.

A parallel may be drawn here with the relation of the pope and the college of bishops. There is a pope because there is a college of bishops, not vice versa, even though the pope's office calls for certain activity in the name of and over the college but never apart from it.

Charism is another approach taken. The many gifts, including ordination, all have their source in the one Spirit. However much they may differ among themselves, they are unified in essence because of their single source. This approach also holds some implications about the recognition, nurturing, and enactment of the charism of priesthood insofar as charisms are understood ordinarily to be for the service of a particular community and sometimes for only a period of time or only in certain circumstances.

A third approach to rethinking lay-clergy relations is to focus on mission, especially as liberative. This orientation concentrates less on the internal constitution and upbuilding of the church and more on the impact of the church on its environment, the world. As the mission of the church is defined concretely, the specific offices and activities which are needed to fulfill the mission are also defined. No matter how much these differ among themselves, they are essentially the same if they flow from and contribute to the one mission of the church.

Of course, it is not easy to agree on what the mission of the church is or what the church needs to do to accomplish that mission or how the mission and internal growth of the church are integrated. Some suggestions were given from the perspective of liberation in the previous chapter and these will be developed more fully in chapters four and five. Nonetheless, the same thrust is found in this approach as in the others: take an inclusive context of which ordination is an integral expression or example but not an essentially different reality.

A similar approach is taken by those who view this question from the perspective of the social sciences. They look upon the church as an organization or system which requires certain offices or roles. These can be quite clearly and distinctly distinguished along with a certain hierarchy of authority and style of decision making. But the unifying factor is the nature of organizations and how they work structurally. There is no basis for claiming an essential difference among the various roles.

This approach may seem to reduce the priesthood to a mere function and to bypass the aspect of personal identification and conformity with Jesus through ordination. The latter is addressed by those who add a cultural-anthropological dimension and focus on the symbolic character of ordained priesthood. The priest is a symbol of what the community as a whole is to be; his life ritualizes the journey of the whole community. Such roles are extremely personal but also integral to the nature of the community whose life they symbolize.

These constructs may not be entirely adequate in themselves but they do complement the theological alternatives and highlight the conviction that ordination should be situated more integrally in an organic, holistic context which acknowledges obvious differences without pushing them to the point of an essential difference. When the latter happens, the history of lay-clergy separation is reenacted and the contrasting experience of ministry becomes an experience of conflict. Historical-critical studies claim freedom for future developments and alternative conceptions help to provide the actual shape of the future. A third approach is just as valuable.

(c) *Symbolic Declericalization*[5]

The painstaking scholarship and careful theologizing represented by the previous two approaches intermingles with some very concrete, practical events that fill out the theological aspect of lay-clergy relations. Clearly the pattern will vary from one place to another, but certain steps have been taken by laity and clergy to declericalize the priesthood, i.e., to overcome in practice the theoretical idea of an essential difference. These steps may be categorized as lifestyle and performance.

Regarding lifestyle perhaps the most significant fact is that there are now many married priests, i.e., ordained priests who have subsequently married. Whether or not these priests have been formally laicized, they are persons who have shared the two dominant lifestyles of the Catholic church—professed celibacy and vowed marriage. As such they represent a blurring of the line between the two, especially if they continue to function in some public, ministerial way.

Celibacy has been the primary practical symbol which conveys the idea of an essential difference, even if theoretically celibacy is not required for ordination. Such a radically different lifestyle signals a radical otherness that is reinforced by special titles, clerical dress, living situation, etc. The necessity for everyone in the church to come to grips with the decisions of priests to marry has done more than anything else to break down the assumed difference between laity and clergy by virtue of ordination.

Accompanying this large-scale sociological shift has been a new, more personable style of interaction between celibate clergy and laity. Clergy more frequently appear in ordinary clothes, visit parishioners informally, go by their first names rather than titles, etc. All this symbolically declericalizes the priesthood and fosters an experience of similarity rather than difference. Needless to say, this declericalizing pattern is not found everywhere and is not necessarily along generational lines. But allowing for the exceptions which can be cited, the informal, personable approach of many priests since Vatican II has helped concretely to overcome the feeling of separation.

Beyond the question of personal styles or preferences, there is also a significant shift in the model and training of priestly candidates. Much more attention today is given to the skills of listening, identifying with others, being present to people without immediately rushing to solutions, conclusions, or assumptions. The priest is supposed to be flexible, creative, adaptive, a servant of the people more than a defender of church practice; a friend more than a director; an enabler more than a controller. The priest's spirituality derives from his active, personal ministry; it is the prime source of his theological and spiritual growth.

The contrast which lay-clergy relations provide for lay ministry has historical, theological, and practical components. These are more easily isolated conceptually than practically for they overlap and influence each other in the course of things. If the previous history of lay-clergy relations has brought us to a period of new lay initiatives, these are being undertaken against the still relevant backdrop of a mixed history and mixed theology. How both of these shape the contrasting experience will be drawn out after taking a closer look at what has been happening practically in lay-clergy relations.

### 3. *Praxis*[6]
At the all-important level of praxis some significant shifts have been occurring in lay-clergy relations. Perhaps the most influential factor of all has been the sudden drop in the number of priests and priest candidates. The most

dramatic decreases were experienced immediately after Vatican II when the largest number of priests resigned from the active ministry and the number of young men entering seminaries dropped off.

One of the effects of this change, as noted in chapter one, has been for clergy, including bishops, to turn to the laity for greater involvement and leadership in the church. As Vatican II reminded everyone, lay persons have the right and responsibility to use their gifts. This may seem like a fortuitous convergence of theory and practice, but not everyone sees it that way.

Many are uncomfortable with the assumption that the role of the laity is affirmed when there is a shortage of priests. Presumably, if there were more priests, there would be fewer lay persons involved in ministry. In addition, others are concerned that the investment in church leadership and activity works against the commitment of the laity to the world. In times of recent social conflict, such as during the war in southeast Asia and the black civil rights movement, it seemed as if the clergy were more concerned with restructuring society while laity were more concerned with restructuring the church along Vatican II reform lines. Such a dichotomy is not desirable, but one result of crossing over the traditional role distinctions is that clergy are more identified with socio-political activities, including a few who hold public office or accept public appointments, while laity are more knowledgeable about the internal workings of the church. The acumen of each group about the other's primary locus has grown. Perhaps it can even lead to a feeling of shared responsibility for the one arena of human life.

Specific issues have fostered this feeling to varying degrees. Abortion has remained the one issue about which laity and clergy alike are in most agreement and willing to take public stands and work for change of public policy. Other issues, such as nuclear weapons, energy conservation, and human rights gain some degree of support. These concerns bring laity and clergy together and forge bonds in praxis that signal a type of cooperative relationship no matter what historical or theoretical factors may threaten that relationship.

The same effect has been experienced in the gradual replacement of a pre-Vatican II parish structure with a post-conciliar structure. It is now quite commonplace to assume that there will be several standing committees in every parish, composed of lay persons who have room to exercise initiative and leadership, if not outright decision-making power. Liturgy, education, social concerns, finance usually have lay representation and input. The coordinating structure for parish life as a whole is the parish council. Despite the mixed results of parish councils so far, the structure itself speaks to a new relationship between laity and clergy.

Within parish life another important structural change is the emergence of full-time, professionally trained lay ministers and the continuation of lay directed renewal movements. Attention has already been drawn to the role of church-professional lay ministers. This phenomenon, which in some ways has achieved what the permanent diaconate has not, is variously interpreted as either a new clericalizing of the laity or a laicizing of the clergy. Whatever the future holds, a new role is taking shape in ministry, and it is altering the perception of what ministry is and what the connection is between ordained and nonordained ministers in praxis.

Renewal movements have had much the same impact.

Capably led by lay persons they have opened up a new experience of leadership and charism in the realm of spirituality. Lay persons prove to be excellent preachers, guides, spiritual directors, prayer leaders. Their ministry not only dispels the assumption that only clergy can provide such services but it raises in a different way the question about ordination and what difference it makes.

These shifts continue to be striking especially to those who were raised before Vatican II. But another sort of contribution is coming from the generation of Catholics who have known only a post-Vatican II church. As these young persons enter adult life, establish families, and take their roles in church and society they bring a different experience of lay-clergy relations from that of their parents. More important, they bring different expectations and are ready to build on the assumption that laity and clergy are called in different ways to share one ministry, to build one church, to fulfill one mission. Some of the battles and tensions of a previous generation are simply nonissues for the current generation.

Another factor at the praxis level is the role of sisters. Technically neither clergy nor laity, religious sisters have been consistently reshaping their role and lifestyle since Vatican II. It is now generally assumed that sisters perform a wide variety of ministries (not just education and health care) and do so in a wide variety of settings, including secular agencies. It is just as customary to expect sisters to live in apartments or homes in neighborhoods rather than in convents on church grounds and to dress basically the same as other women in society. All this has helped provide a new experience of the religious and a new working relationship with the laity, although these very changes create tension and discomfort in some parts of the church (especially it seems at the Vatican).

A final area of praxis is worth noting. In the preparation of seminarians for ordination today, the field education program is extremely important. This often means that a seminarian works in a parish or a hospital or agency where he meets laity in a ministerial capacity. Because he does not have the full role of priest or deacon, the seminarian is in a unique position to test and shape his identity against the expectations of the laity he meets. In addition, the laity have some sense that they are helping to shape the priestly style of the future.

Although formal lay involvement in field education is negligible in Roman Catholic circles compared to formation in Protestant churches, there is at least more likelihood of exposure and contact with laity during the formative period than was the case in the past. In addition, the average age of seminarians today is two to five years older than the age at which a previous generation was ordained. This means that candidates for priesthood are bringing a more extensive experience *as* lay persons to their formation. This often includes professional training and work experience in another field. The long-range impact of this fact for lay-clergy relations is hard to predict, but the future clergy should be more in touch with the feelings and experience of the laity than clergy in the past.

The foregoing factors are all basically positive. They enhance the sense of intimacy and cooperation and unity between laity and clergy. There are, to be sure, numerous factors and examples to the contrary. They may even dominate. The point here is that there are significant, structural changes at the practical level which have had some impact already and should continue to do so. The impact is in the area of changing the *experience* of laity-clergy relations.

Indeed, all three elements identified so far in the lay-

clergy contrast speak to a change, an opening, a freeing
without defining too precisely or too absolutely what those
changes, openings, freedoms are. And this is perhaps the
central contrasting experience which lay-clergy relations
contribute to the dominant experience of lay ministry.
Lines cannot be drawn neatly or clearly between laity and
clergy. Lay ministry occurs in a dynamic, fluid relationship
with ordained ministry. Both are being redefined, restyled,
reshaped simultaneously and together. Lay-clergy relations
provide an environment or field within which lay ministry
occurs and from which lay ministry derives a more intense
character and a more extensive importance.

## World-Church Relations

The experience of lay ministry is set within another contrasting context: the world-church relationship. The contrast here has two aspects. One is the long-standing association of clergy with ministry in the church and laity with
ministry in the world. The second is the recent reversal of
these roles among some clergy which has raised questions
about who is responsible for what and how absolutely the
roles of laity and clergy should be defined. In order to
sharpen this contrast, it is helpful to examine three aspects
of the situation: the general relationship of world and
church as described at Vatican II and in major church pronouncements since Vatican II; the secularity of the laity;
and the rationale for clergy taking active roles in the socio-
political sphere of society. From this cluster of reflections
some synthesis of the world-church contrast can be drawn.

### 1. *Vatican II*

One of the primary purposes for which Pope John
XXIII convened the Second Vatican Council was to im-

prove the church's relations with the modern world. Those relations had become gradually more positive after the adamant, separatist position of Pius IX in the nineteenth century. Beginning with Leo XIII, the Vatican addressed itself more constructively to the modern world. The shift was slow and appears to be a significant change only in the hindsight of some seventy-five years or more.

The shift is characterized by an effort to speak to very concrete problems (wages, working conditions, unions, property rights) in a way that might be heard, especially by persons who are not Roman Catholic. In this regard, notable progress is discernible, culminating with the fresh spirit of goodwill engendered by John XXIII.

The major social encyclical of John's pontificate, *Mater et Magistra,* struck a new chord in Vatican statements about the modern world. There was an unmistakable tone of openness and cooperation that put the church in the posture of an ally and concerned citizen rather than a judge or aloof observer. This feeling not only exemplified John XXIII's own image but it also reinforced the tendencies found in many contemporary authors to strike a new, positive appreciation of the modern world. Foremost among these authors was Teilhard de Chardin whose writings were becoming more widely available at the time of Vatican II.

All this set the mood for a conciliar look at the world. However, the initial set of concerns on the Council's agenda did not include an explicit treatment of world-church relations. This was partly because church concerns seemed more urgent to the bishops and other council leaders, but it was also partly because John XXIII had issued a second major encyclical on a social issue—peace (in *Pacem in Terris).* With two significant (and well-received) papal documents on current social problems, the Council felt reluctant to take up the same issues. It might even seem an affront for the Council to address questions which the pope had just spoken about—a hierarchical mentality still very dominant in 1962.

Hence, despite his urging and his own initiatives, Pope John found that the Council was bypassing the issue which figured so forcefully in his own decision to convene the bishops and religious leaders in the first place. That is when he prevailed upon Cardinal Suenens, who had earlier published a pastoral letter on world-church relations which caught Pope John's attention, to intervene in the Council proceedings and call for a new document. Cardinal Suenens did so in his famous speech of December 1, 1962. The speech was seconded by Cardinal Montini, who would be pope by the next session. Thus was born the document which became the Pastoral Constitution on the Church in the Modern World.

This Pastoral Constitution is unique among conciliar documents, not only because of its genesis, but also because it departs from high church vocabulary and is willing to admit that the church is limited in its contribution to solving the world's problems. The posture of a collaborator that knows its own identity and specific contribution fostered a new style of relating to the world. Its impact was not lost on church members themselves, especially not on the clergy. A new spirit emerged, fueled by the Pastoral Constitution on the Church in the Modern World.

Underlying the spirit and tone of the document was a reclaiming of the theology of incarnation which had been developing in the Roman Catholic church for the previous several generations. Incarnational theology gives full weight to the human, the historical, and the eschatological or future dimension of Christian faith.

The human dimension prizes the accomplishments of human society as a genuine development of God's creation but does not shy away from acknowledging new problems and questions which those very accomplishments engender. The church is not the only agency concerned about this, for persons of goodwill everywhere struggle to create a better world. But a theological affirmation of human dignity and potential capitalizes on the best parts of the Catholic tradition and reinforces the connection between world and church, laity and clergy rather than the separation between them. This emphasis creates some ambiguity about where the world leaves off and the church begins, a question that has direct bearing on the roles of laity and clergy.

The historical dimension of incarnational theology introduces a self-critical aspect into the church's reflections and proposals for social action. In the ecumenical quest for unity, the church has shown a willingness to acknowledge its own shortcomings and to review its own development. The same self-critical spirit spurs discussion regarding world-church relations. At the Council this was most sharply evident on the question of religious liberty. The church clearly stood on the principle of freedom while accepting the fact of pluralism which defines social life today. Unwilling to dictate that life, the church is equally unwilling to be excluded from making its contribution to it.

The eschatological dimension of incarnational theology requires openness to the future as God's arena of activity, but at the same time it requires distance from the contributions which the church can make to that future. Eschatology prevents the church from thinking that it must do everything on its own or from doing nothing and waiting for God to act. Eschatology lends ultimate importance to the decisions and policies of the present because the future emerges from the present and to some degree is conditioned by it.

These general reflections and shifts of attitude were put to the test in the U.S. through the civil rights movement and the war in southeast Asia. Such major social events demanded a response from every citizen. Catholics were trying to respond precisely at the time that the basic attitude and praxis of the church toward society was changing. It was not a time for disengaged reflection. Action often preceded careful theorizing.

In the midst of all this, additional official statements were issued, most notably Pope Paul VI's encyclical on the Development of Peoples, the 1971 Bishops Synod statement on Justice in the World, and the highly publicized meeting of the Latin American bishops at Medellin. All these pronouncements pushed the church further toward a deep, integral commitment to the world. How that commitment was to be carried out remained an open question, but *that* such a commitment was intrinsic to a Christian's vocation was no longer deniable.

The Second Vatican Council had begun to reconceptualize and reexperience the world. The upshot of this effort was a more open-ended, mutually influencing, collaborative relationship between the church and the world. The pluralistic differences were acknowledged as both real and irremovable. The task was to discover, together, how to work to guarantee human rights, human development, and human fulfillment. The church maintained a stout confidence that it had an indispensible contribution to make to this effort. The church's contribution draws upon its own sources but relates to the world as it actually exists, without demanding that some other kind of world be put in place first or without abandoning the present world for another one, yet to come.

Some unforeseen results have accompanied this development. The self-critical edge toward society has become divisive within the church. Laity and clergy are sometimes split among themselves about the relative importance of social justice in the church's mission and even more so on specific tactics for achieving social justice. Moreover, the same self-critical bent has been directed at the church precisely as an institution regarding the role of women, unionization of church workers, investment of funds, rights within the church, etc.

In addition, there has been uneven response to different social issues. Whereas abortion and nuclear war have had widespread attention (if not support), other issues have had mixed or little response.

In the midst of all this, there has been a consistent commitment to provide social services to the needy. But here another line of division appears between those who try to meet immediate needs and those who want to go beyond that to effect structural change. The result is at times a fragmented effort within the church. Unwilling to settle for less than comprehensive service, the church has found itself thinned, splintered, and wearied in trying to carry through a new relation to the world.

## 2. *The Secularity of the Laity*[8]

The Second Vatican Council initiated a new relationship between the church and the world. That relationship includes a new appreciation of the secular dimension of human experience. This has implications for the identity of the laity and lay ministry.

The first significant attempt in modern times to assess positively the secularity of the laity came through Catholic Action (as described in the introduction and earlier in this chapter). But the primary orientation of Catholic Action was pragmatic. The hierarchy wanted to influence the modern world but were unable to do so directly because too large a gap and too great an antipathy had developed between the official church and the world. The laity, however, were already in the world in the sense that they were primarily identified with secular life rather than ecclesiastical or vowed religious life. Their secularity had a utilitarian value. It was a ready-made link between church and world.

The laity who responded to Catholic Action tended to be extensions of the clergy, doing in the world what the clergy would have done if they could have had the same access. Although Catholic Action did give the laity a new status and a new role in the mission of the church, it did not fully appreciate the value of their secularity. Instead of becoming a new source of theology and ministry because of their secular existence, the laity became a new medium for transmitting the established theology and ministry of the clergy (as in the first model of Leonard Doohan cited in chapter one).

This condition was still quite dominant at the beginning of Vatican II and throughout its sessions. But in the course of those sessions some shifts began to occur. The secularity of the laity was slowly being recognized, not just as a fortuitous piece of strategy for the clergy, but as a gift in its own right. Moreover, it is a gift which the laity themselves possess and are best able to enunciate and implement. Gradually, a feeling of relative autonomy or interdependence has been emerging which greatly enhances the possibility of a liberative lay ministry (as indicated in chapter two).

What has the secularity of the laity come to mean? It has meant an additional and alternative source of theological insight and practical action to that of the clergy. It has meant an increasingly adult laity who claim their adulthood in matters religious as well as secular (as the bishops noted in *Called and Gifted*). Probably the clearest example of what this means was the response to Pope Paul VI's teaching on artificial contraception.

Here was an issue that affected married lay persons in a direct way. It was full of religious, psychological, sociological, medical, spiritual, cultural, and numerous other dimensions. It was an issue on which the laity as a whole, together with the clergy, were coming to some consensus. When the pope issued his encyclical, it was clear that an adult laity received it.

Faced with an apparent crisis, lay persons made their decisions in light of their interpretation of what was at stake. Some left the organized church, others dissented and remained, still others conformed freely and some conformed unwillingly. The point is not who was right and who was wrong but rather that lay persons responded with a freedom of conscience and autonomous spirit characteristic of adults who ultimately rely on their own experience and wisdom. (A similar example exists currently with the reception of the new Code of Canon Law, although the issues here are generally less immediate in the lives of lay people.)

The real meaning of the laity's secularity is that they have gifts of insight, special grace of discernment, special authority for action precisely because they are in the secular sphere. They are preeminently the incarnational church. Called to witness to the gospel in the world, they do not rely totally or even primarily on the clergy for answers or guidance or approval. They have their own sources within their secular experience. This is the deepest meaning of the laity's secularity (and it will be elaborated in chapter five).

This is not to say that the clergy have nothing to contribute. It is rather a question of redefining and repositioning the role of the clergy. As persons trained in the tradition of the church and representative of the official teaching and its ongoing tradition, clergy are a valuable resource to the laity, not as controllers but as contributors. In practice, it hasn't always come out this way. The clergy agenda is still usually dominant and laity are invited to share in it.

On the other hand, clergy sometimes have a better insight into the secularity of the laity than the laity do. An "outsider" can often enlighten a person's situation precisely as an outsider, from a creative and fruitful distance. In fact, this perspective has led some clergy to move into roles typically associated with the laity. This will be taken up in the next section. The point here is that there is more to the secularity of the laity than is usually recognized, far more than Catholic Action saw and even more than Vatican II saw. The freedom and contribution of the laity's experience in the world is a source of theology and ministry which only the laity can provide, and they will do so only if their secularity is prized for what it is.

### 3. *Secularizing of the Clergy*

The general blurring of lines between church and world which has resulted from Vatican II is concretized in the activity of those clergy who move into secular roles as an extension of their ministry. Although the actual number of priests and sisters who hold public office, serve in leadership positions in government or civic agencies, form organizations for social import, etc., remains quite small, their impact on the consciousness of the church and the public is quite large.

In addition to activists on the civil rights front, peace movement, farmworkers strikes, and other social causes, there is a significant, vocal group of clergy who take clear positions on social issues in their preaching and ministry. The response of the laity seems mixed. There is the usual chorus of opposition when clergy do or say anything political, because it is assumed that this is outside the pale of the clergy's competence or role. Others are more selective, supporting the involvement of clergy in certain issues (such as abortion) but not in others (such as military spending). Still others see the direct involvement of clergy in these areas as disregarding the laity and evidencing a bias against working for change from within systems (as noted in the Chicago Declaration of Concern in chapter one).

All in all, the involvement of clergy in areas of secular life raises more questions for the laity than for the clergy. What is the role of the laity in the world? How do they exercise their Christian values? Where do they get support and what forms does it take? What resources do they need and where will they get them? How dependent on church officials are they in acting *as* Christians and in the name of the church? How important is it to act in the name of the church if one is acting in the name of Christ? What are the unique opportunities laity have and what risks do they face in fulfilling those opportunities? Do they feel themselves part of the church at such times?

These questions are properly put to the laity, not because the *laity* have been negligent or deficient or out of step up till now, but because these are church questions. They are questions which define in practice what the church is as the continuation of Jesus' life in the world. Because the laity are at the very heart of the church in the world, it is both consistent and correct to ask these essential church questions in terms of the laity's experience and ministry first of all. The fact that this is not ordinarily done is not an indictment of the laity but an indication of previous, misdirected priorities.

To sum up. The dominant experience of the laity since Vatican II has been the experience of ministry. That experience is set in the twin contrasts of lay-clergy relations and world-church relations. As both sets of relations have developed since Vatican II, they have intensified and enlarged the experience of lay ministry.

Vis-à-vis the clergy, lay ministry represents a new historical moment and an experience which goes deeper to the foundation of Christian life than ordained ministry. Vis-à-vis the world, lay ministry represents a new source of theology and ministry, one that is interdependent with the hierarchical church but also more autonomous than in the past. The total experience of lay ministry since Vatican II calls for a new symbol which can express these dominant and contrasting aspects and point in the direction of new, fruitful experience. Such a symbol is proposed and analyzed in the next chapter.

# CHAPTER FOUR

## Symbolization:
## The Care of Society

AFTER analyzing the experience of lay persons since Vatican II, it is time to put it all together. This is a creative and speculative step. It moves from an interpretation of what has been happening to a projection of what could happen in the future. However, the projection emerges *from* the interpretation; it is not imposed from the outside or introduced arbitrarily. The past is the stuff out of which the future evolves.

In making a shift like this from analysis to synthesis, from the past to the future, symbols are especially valuable. As used here, a symbol brings together in one image both the dominant and contrasting factors which have been identified in the previous analysis. When this happens, the symbol also transforms the previous material and opens up new possibilities for action.

Thus, a symbol functions in several ways at once. It unifies; it transforms; it leads to new action. Of course, all this happens only if the symbol itself is right, and that is not always easy to determine. A symbol may seem to have a lot of potential at first but turn out not to be as useful as anticipated. Something like this has occurred with the symbol 'team ministry.' This image was widely invoked for a while to describe a new style of ministering. But experience has shown in many instances that ministers don't live or work as a team so much as they just communicate better about what they're doing.

On the other hand, a symbol that feels right conceptu-

ally may not contribute much experientially. An example
of this is the symbol of the 'presider' at worship. This term
has an ancient history and suggests a different understanding of the priest's role, but it need not change at all the way
a priest actually carries out that role.

So symbols generate some ambiguity and can fall flat
when they are put into practice. But the risks are certainly
worth the results when a symbol works. And a symbol
works when it entices people to enter into it, to perceive
themselves as part of it, and to project a course of conduct
out of it. That is the intention behind the symbol I would
like to propose for lay ministry. That symbol is 'the care of
society.'

As a synthesis of the dominant experience of ministry
and the contrasts of lay-clergy relations and church-world
relations, the care of society is composed of two familiar
concepts: pastoral care and society. The combination of
these concepts, especially as a symbol of the experience of
lay ministry, points to a new possibility for understanding
and exercising lay ministry in the future. The purpose of
this chapter is to spell out what the symbol means and to
show how it synthesizes the material of chapters one, two,
and three. The purpose of the next chapter is to set out
some of the implications of the symbol for enactment.

### Pastoral Care[1]

Pastoral care has a venerable image in Christian history.
It is rooted in biblical references which express the attitude, motive, and style of ministry right up to our own
day. The dominant image of Vatican II was that of a *pastoral* council rather than a dogmatic or disciplinary council. The precise meaning of "pastoral" in this context was
never really defined nor should it have been, because the

word pastoral was used to convey a feeling, a sensitivity, an experience of being church.

Instead of a council (and church) that issues dogmatic pronouncements or sets up rules of conduct, a pastoral council (and church) exhibits in the first place a genuine concern for people. Dogmas and discipline come later. Pastoral concern or care is aimed at people in the real circumstances of their daily lives. It is responsive, concrete, open to what's happening.

It should be no surprise then that a pastoral council like Vatican II responded to the needs of its own members by making the liturgy more accessible, by endorsing Scripture study and devotion, by supporting the ecumenical movement, by reaffirming traditional commitments to education, mission, seminary training, indeed, by speaking for the first time in a conciliar document about the laity themselves.

It should be also no surprise that such a pastoral council would respond to the needs of people everywhere by declaring its support for religious liberty and its cooperation with all people of goodwill in working for a better world. Interestingly, the council's major statement on the church and the modern world was the only document of Vatican II to be called a *pastoral* constitution.

This spirit of concern and desire to respond to people in their real situations has continued since Vatican II. In the U.S. alone, the bishops and the agencies of the bishops conference have issued numerous pastoral letters, pastoral plans, and pastoral reflections. And these references are only a small part of the total outpouring of material, organizations, programs, and activities that are characterized as pastoral. In all of this, however, this term is invoked much more widely and frequently than it is defined clearly or precisely. This indicates again that the term pastoral (like the term ministry) refers primarily to an experience, a sensitivity, a feeling.

That feeling is linked up with our experience of God's care for us as that divine care has been manifested in history and recorded especially in the Scriptures. When our Jewish ancestors looked for a symbol that would express how God cared for them, they frequently referred to the shepherd, the pastor.

Jesus used the same motif to describe his service to the people even though he was not, strictly speaking, a shepherd. Some of the earliest Christian literature offered advice or exhortation in the same way—as a shepherd caring for a flock. When different offices emerged in the structure of the church (as noted in chapter three), especially the office of overseer or bishop, the duties of the office holders were described by using the model of a shepherd.

Leaders of Christian communites were expected to fulfill their roles like shepherds because that was the primary model provided by Jesus. Why has this model endured, even in cultural settings like ours where shepherds are not present? Basically because the *qualities* of a shepherd are the fundamental qualities expected of anyone who would care as Jesus did and because shepherds were and are real, even if they are not part of our direct experience. The qualities of a shepherd are not mere ideals which no one has ever lived out. They are the characteristics of flesh and blood persons.

A shepherd is responsible for providing nourishment for the sheep, for protecting them from danger and enemies, and for keeping them together. In short, a shepherd cares for the whole life of the sheep. In order to fulfill this responsibility, a shepherd has to know the sheep and be with them. No one can shepherd from a distance or only now and then. Being a shepherd implies a commitment, a relationship to the sheep. And there are risks. If danger presents itself, a shepherd personally becomes the defense of the sheep. In short, a shepherd is dedicated to the sheep and finds personal satisfaction in caring for them.

These are the same qualities which are expected of pastoral carers. Unfortunately, the corresponding qualities of sheep have been carried along and applied to the communities (i.e., the laity) which pastors minister to. Unlike a flock of sheep, however, Christian believers are not dependent, utterly helpless, dumb animals who, in the words of one experienced pastor, are good only for fleecing and eating. The negative and inappropriate identification of sheep with laity does not mean that the qualities of a shepherd are inappropriate for ministry.

In fact, in recent pastoral care literature the image of the shepherd has been given renewed prominence, not just for the ordained minister, but for all believers who care. Even in literature which is critical of certain trends in modern pastoral care, the image of the shepherd is upheld as the appropriate model or symbol. Of course, works which discuss the traditional office of the ordained minister also make ample use of the shepherd image.

All of this discussion points to the continued relevance of the shepherd as a prime image for understanding and carrying out ministry. This image is especially applicable if the qualities of shepherding are stressed rather than the specific acts of shepherding (pastoral care in its classic sense of ordained ministry). Those qualities are primarily affective, consisting of a genuine feeling of concern for others which prompts a response to their needs.

This feeling of concern may appropriately be described

in terms of freedom or liberation. The one who exercises pastoral care aims at creating conditions or offering service which will enable those cared for to be liberated, as far as possible, from controlling or limiting circumstances. The final choices and shaping of experience rests with those cared for; the carer tries to maximize the potential for the other(s) to live in a free, personal, self-determining way.

This does not mean that the carer is a neutral observer, only influencing the environment in which others live. A pastoral carer exerts influence by establishing a relationship, by entering into the life experience of others. But the pastoral carer does not usurp the ultimate freedom of others to control their lives. This is the delicate balance and art of pastoral care—to be involved without interfering; to be caring without controlling. To do so effectively requires great self-discipline by the pastoral carer. It also requires skill.

It is not enough to feel for others and want to help them. A pastoral carer is also a skilled carer or skilled helper (as noted in chapter two). Proper skills temper the tendency to intervene too quickly or take over for others when they might better take care of themselves. The specific skills needed will vary, depending on the needs of those being cared for, but the general point is that genuine pastoral care is a blending of feeling and skill. To overemphasize feeling may not result in effective care; to overemphasize skills may reduce pastoral care to a set of clinical techniques.

The balance and skill that is required for effective pastoral care has sometimes reinforced the idea that only professionally trained, official ministers are the true agents of pastoral care. Because the word pastoral has been so closely identified with the office of pastor, or ordained minister, the care which all Christians are to give is not usually thought of as pastoral care. This tendency has been resisted in some recent writing which speaks explicitly of lay pastoral care and describes some practical ways of acquiring the skills needed to offer such care effectively.

This is an encouraging direction, because the qualities of being a shepherd, a pastoral carer are deeply imbedded in the Christian tradition. In addition, they are precisely the qualities which describe how many lay persons feel who are drawn to respond to others in a caring, helping, effective way. Also, pastoral care more readily conveys the affective dimension of service than the word ministry does. Care orients one to a feeling-for others more than a doing-for others, and in that respect it may even get closer to the essence of what ministry is. Pastoral care focuses on experience; it highlights the person-centered nature of ministry, and it calls for the skills to do ministry effectively. All this is true of pastoral care as it is traditionally understood. What does it mean when coupled with society?

## Care of Society[2]

The usual context for pastoral care is interpersonal relationships within a Christian community, usually a parish. These may be one-to-one relationships as in counseling or personal visits, or they may be small group or community relationships, as in a divorced and single parent group. Such specific, highly personal situations call for particular abilities, such as listening skills, empathic responses, consensus building, conflict resolution, and so on.

Pastoral care is not ordinarily used to describe activity in the context of society. When political, economic, military, or cultural issues are the focus of a religious response, the response is described in terms of social ethics, peace and justice, social mission, or outreach, but not pastoral care. Pastoral care traditionally tends to be confined to the caring that goes on within and among church members.

Despite this customary restriction of the term, pastoral care has a rich enough meaning to be extended to the societal context. The care of society cares for the spirit of society; it seeks to nurture its vitality, respond to its needs, and support its possibilities, all within an overarching commitment to liberation. The care of society aims at creating the conditions of freedom that will facilitate the praxis of liberation at the three levels described in chapter two.

The care of society is not so much a set of concrete goals or a stategy for achieving them. Rather it is a sensitive, feeling-with and feeling-for the society in which we live. It expresses the feeling and care which God has for the created order. The ultimate origin of the care of society, therefore, is our faith, our living relationship with God from which we derive our sense of the world. If the care of society remains true to its source, it will not become mere social activism.

The basic qualities which pastoral care traditionally emphasizes are the same qualities required for the care of society. The major difference is that the care of society includes larger social groupings than interpersonal or small group relationships, and it also includes social systems and policies as well as persons. The essential qualities of pastoral care, when carried over to society, may be grouped as follows.

### 1. *Investment*

The indispensible basis for the care of society is a willingness to invest oneself in caring for society. This is the same quality of commitment, acceptance, and love which grounds all pastoral care and makes it something other than clinical assistance. There are usually mixed motives which prompt a person's investment in another. There is a certain degree of self-satisfaction that comes with helping others. Few people can maintain a personal investment in others if they get nothing out of it for themselves. This is not selfishness; it is being human. People need to grow and experience and mature in what they do. Otherwise, they become cynical or tend to burnout.

But few people would ever even begin to invest themselves in others if they didn't feel, at some level, that the persons being cared for are valuable, have some potential, are worth the effort, call out to them, indeed claim them. This feeling is sometimes hard to explain to others. There are many who dedicate themselves to apparently hopeless causes and persist in their efforts despite few discernible successes. When asked why, they will usually respond, "If I can help just one person, it's worth it; someone has to try; we can't just abandon these people."

Behind such statements is a profound feeling that we are all bound to one another all the time. We are not first individuals who choose to come together to form groups and community and society (even though this is the political theory on which our form of government rests). We are from the beginning interdependent, social beings whose individuality emerges in relationship to others. We carry this feeling of interdependence within us, even when we assert our individual autonomy at times. Our sense of interdependence conditions how we feel about ourselves and others. We are unavoidably linked to one another so that to be uncaring of others is ultimately to be uncaring of ourselves, even if we are not always conscious of that fact.

The care of society calls for investment in society out of

the same awareness and motivation. We care for society
not out of benevolence or even out of choice, as if there
were a true alternative. Rather we care for society out of
the recognition that we *are* society; we *are* the world we
create together. To the degree that this view is not preval-
ent in our current society, the care of society has a countercultural cast to it.

The acknowledgement that we are society parallels a
familiar claim since Vatican II; namely, we are the church.
As used in post-Vatican II discussions, this phrase means
that, by initiation into Jesus, we are all united as one people whom we call church. The same life is shared by all and
with all. And just as important, the life that is shared is
*already there* before anyone of us is initiated into it. First
there is the church, the life of Christ; then there are individual members. Members are truly individuals; they do
not lose their unique identities. But they are always members *of* the church of Christ. The individual members do
not constitute the church in the sense that they could all get
together and decide to decompose it, to annihilate it, to
stop its existence permanently. The church of Christ depends on its members for the quality of its existence but
not for the fact of its existence. Similarly, it is the communal, organic life of the church that makes possible the
achievements of growth and grace, insight and holiness of
the individual members. We belong to the church as much
as the church belongs to us. We have been trying to learn
what this means in concrete, practical terms since Vatican
II, but it is *this* vision of church that we are trying to learn
and live out.

What is true of the church through initiation is also true
of social life through birth. The communal life of the
church is not a totally unique experience within creation. It

is an explicit expression of what is fundamentally true of all life. We are first related to everyone and everything else and in those relations we become the individuals we are. There is in fact great scope for individual becoming within the social relatedness of human existence, but the most basic truth is that social relatedness is primary and a condition for individual emergence.

This, at any rate, is the view which is at the heart of the care of society. It presumes an awareness of our societal interdependence which makes personal investment in society worth it. This presumption is constantly challenged, of course. Many times and in many respects society does not seem to be worth a personal investment. It does not seem to offer a sufficient value or potential for one's own growth or the growth of others, especially those who are treated unjustly or neglected. The same challenge arises in the pastoral care of individuals. Many times and in many respects individuals do not seem to be worth the investment.

At such times it is essential to know and affirm the foundation for caring. Care of any type is sustained, not because of a higher percentage of "successful cases" (the pragmatic motive), but because of the profound feeling-for the worth of others and the inseparable bonds among us, bonds which are there even before we meet, bonds which claim us even before we make conscious choices (the intrinsic motive).

These bonds are not arbitrary or unfair or self-denying. They are like the bonds of family or love or attraction. They spell out the givenness of life, the fact that we emerge in a context which is already there, which claims us and which we contribute to. To view society only as something we take from or use for our private purposes is ultimately to deny reality itself and to work against the fullest personal experience we could have.

The care of society, like the pastoral care of individuals, implies investment. This is a feeling-for the intrinsic value of society which in turn is grounded in the awareness that we are all interdependent. Out interdependence is expressed socially and claims our care for society because we are first of all social beings.

## 2. *Discernment*

The second quality of the care of society is discernment. This means a realistic, discriminating interpretation of society, an understanding of how it has developed, how it presently functions, and what it could become. Without such discrimination, the care of society could lapse into a naive romanticism that would not be able to *care* for society in the manner of caring described earlier in this chapter. The care of society is a deep, genuine feeling-for society seasoned with experience and judgment.

The parallel in the pastoral care of individuals is the listening skill and empathic response which help to disclose what is really going on in the life of an individual and where that movement can lead. Without such skill and the willingness, at times the risk, to use it, liberative care is not likely to occur.

The same is true for the care of society. There are skills needed to disclose what is really going on in society. Generally, these are the skills of social analysis which enable people to hear, feel, see, and get in touch with what is happening in society and where that can lead. Such skills may be highly developed, as in centers of professional analysis, or may be part of the common wisdom that guides citizens in communities everywhere.

In addition, society will be analyzed quite differently by persons with the same professional training or life experience. And, of course, different social issues (economy, military, education . . .) will require different areas of expertise or familiarity. Society is complex and pluralistic; discernment of society will be too. Uniformity is not the goal but discernment, a discernment that leads to the most liberative care of society which present reality allows for. That is not always easy to determine.

In a pluralistic society like ours, the accumulation of data to be taken into account can seem overwhelming. This leads some to leave decisions only to experts because they themselves feel so incompetent. Or it can prompt some to feel cynical or fatalistic because "not much changes anyway, so why bother?" Or it can lead to a withdrawal into mere privatism, as if the social context really doesn't exert that much influence on one's life. The point of the care of society is that society cannot be taken for granted. The quality and potential of societal life hinge on the decisions and actions of its members.

The same tendencies to back off appear in the pastoral care of individuals. Such care can be so overprofessionalized that only experts (the ordained or credentialed) are supposed to do it. Or a pastoral carer who has been at it for several years can develop the attitude that certain problems never go away and certain people never change, so what's the use? There is also a type of withdrawal, usually associated with burnout, when a person avoids care situations in order to get on with "one's own" life or ministry.

Pastoral care of any type can verge into overspecialization, make more of problems than is really there, or it can lapse into cynicism and stereotypes, imposing previous experience on new situations and disregarding the potential for change and improvement. Unless the skills of pastoral care are constantly wrapped in the feeling-for the value of those cared for, any of these tendencies can develop. The same is true for the care of society.

The care of society invests in society skillfully. It is neither naive nor cynical. It attends to the present, remembers the past, envisions the future. It is always discerning what is going on and where that can lead. Where it can lead is couched within the possibilities of society as it actually exists. So the care of society takes present reality very seriously, just as the pastoral care of individuals takes the present situation of individuals very seriously. Present reality is not the limit of what might be but the starting point for discerning what else might be.

The focus of the discernment of the care of society is the spirit of society. This is essentially a spirit of social awareness and feeling-for our interdependence. How this appears or does not appear in specific situations is the initial question. How it can be nurtured (where it appears) or how it can be introduced (where it does not appear) is the next question. The assumption of the care of society is that if the value of social life and the feeling-for interdependence is kept clear, then the decisions and policies that are needed to foster freedom in society will more likely follow. This is not naive optimism; it is critical realism.

### 3. *Measurement*

The third quality of the care of society is measurement. This means that the care offered is measured by the circumstances in which it occurs. The care of society is respectful of limitations. Recognizing that social life is interdependent does not mean that everything, in all its ramifications, must be dealt with all the time. In fact, the opposite is the case.

In the pastoral care of individuals many factors are operative simultaneously. Using listening skills and empathic responses, a pastoral carer must discern which of these is primary and how it affects the others. Usually the key in individual pastoral care is to take what is presented by the individual as the starting point. This may not be the most important issue ultimately, but it expresses where the individual actually is and it is eventually connected to the most important issue.

The connection is an indication of interdependence within individuals. The same is true in society. Everything is interconnected. The care of society begins with what a particular social situation presents as its need or problem or possibility. The situation is the measure of the care that is offered. To care for society in this way is to respect what is given, limited as it may be at first.

The limitation gives way soon enough. Every measured contribution inevitably touches other, related situations or aspects of societal life. These may become the focus of a subsequent effort of care. The point is that care of society always has society as a whole in the background while focusing on some immediate concern, just as the pastoral care of individuals has the individual as a whole in the background while focusing on some immediate concern of the individual. This dual focus does not mean that limited, immediate needs are never met because there is always a bigger problem or possibility connected to it. Care of society means this limited, immediate need is met with a view toward this need leading to other, related issues.

This raises the related question of when to move from

one issue to another, when to intervene with one's own discernment of what is important next. This is part of the art as well as the skill of the care of society. There is no infallible guide for knowing. It is part of the discernment mentioned above, and it is part of keeping aware of the whole. It is always possible to hold back too much or to move ahead too fast or too far. This is part of the risk of caring for society. It is also its discipline and prophecy.

To care for society within the limits given by a certain situation calls for a discipline of one's own instincts and desires which may not in fact respect reality as it is given in this particular situation. At the same time, the care of society should be prophetic, willing to go beyond the given and generate something really new. The care of society is not meant to be conformist, certainly not in the sense of merely endorsing the status quo. It is prophetic in the sense of always nurturing the possibilities for new life as these emerge from the stubborn facts of life. This form of measured prophecy is freeing, in contrast to a dogmatic stance which imposes a singular view of how societal life should be in given circumstances and tries to make reality fit that view.

The care of society is interactive and interdependent. It discerns with and through society as it is given, not to keep it that way but to free it for a fuller realization. Its prophecy, like its care, is measured.

The care of society means an investment in society which is made with a discerning sensitivity and is measured by the actual conditions which define social reality. This general description of the symbol raises two crucial questions: Who is to do this and what will it take to do it? The answer to the first question is that the laity are the prime carers of society. What it will take to do so will be discussed in chapter five.

## The Care of Society as Lay Ministry

The care of society is a symbol. It aims at synthesizing the dominant and contrasting elements in the experience of lay persons since Vatican II and in doing so it also aims at new directions for lay ministry. How does the care of society do this?

The dominant factor in the postconciliar experience of the laity is ministry. As developed in chapter two, the key to understanding ministry is liberation. Liberation is understood as threefold: human sustenance, human dignity, and human salvation. The widespread acceptance and use of the term ministry to describe the dominant movement of lay activity points to three interlocking strands of meaning ranging from importance to authenticity, from equality to complementarity, from ownership to partnership. The care of society expresses each of these strands while affirming the core meaning of ministry as liberation, as a caring response to others according to the shepherding model of Jesus which frees people to fulfill their potential. Pastoral care has consistently endorsed the qualities of this caring response, qualities which should characterize the activity of all Christians.

Care of society expresses both ends of the continuum from importance to authenticity. Nothing can be more important than to care for others as Jesus did. This means to feel a genuine commitment to others, to be willing to invest in them even at personal risk. When a person arrives at this level of commitment, the ministry is not only important but authentic. It does not derive from someone else's mandate or approval. It is coming from the very source of Christian life itself.

Care of society also expresses the poles of equality and complementarity. Care is primarily other-oriented; it does not depend on the status or preference of the carer. The quality of care is the issue, and this equalizes all those who offer it. More than this, the care of society seeks the best care, the most extensive liberation for others, and that means drawing upon all the resources available. Different gifts or experiences or opportunities are seen as complementary when other persons are seen as the focus of the care. When this is so, the relative status of the carer fades out of the picture, and the maximum qualitative service emerges.

Finally, the care of society affirms the value of ownership and partnership because the liberation that occurs in ministry results from relationships, and people make up relationships. Unless people own their gifts, their experiences, their values, their feelings, they can't do much relational ministry. Likewise, until people enter partnerships to strengthen one another and care together, they won't be very effective in society.

All of these qualities are traditionally associated with pastoral care. The care of society draws upon this tradition of meaning but uses it to express and affirm what is already operative in the lay experience. The care of society does not transpose the lay experience into a narrower context of church organization and structure in order to derive its meaning or value.

It is true that the tradition of pastoral care is closely associated with the work of the pastor, the ordained minister. This association leads to a restriction of the term pastoral care, which in turn has two misleading impressions. One is that only when the ordained minister acts does "the church" act; the other is that the church (in this restricted sense) has no direct role to play in society.

An indication of both points may be seen in the use of language. In general discussion since Vatican II the laity are commonly and comfortably referred to as "the church." But when lay persons engage in direct action on behalf of justice in society, their activity is usually called Christian witness or social responsibility or even social ministry, but it is not described as the action of "the church." Whereas, mere teachings with no immediate, practical impact are routinely referred to as the social teaching of "the church."

There is a long history behind this overidentification of the church with the ordained and an even longer history of the separation of the church and the world. There is also some validity to the role of designated leaders (like the ordained) to represent the whole body of people in a way that ordinary members don't. These are real factors which complicate the meaning of the term pastoral care when it is used in the symbol, care of society. Nonetheless, the term is valuable because it says what lay ministry is about, although it can say that only if the more primal and primary meaning of shepherding is stressed. If the term pastoral care remains wedded to its biblical origins, its inclusive, affective range of meaning, then it can serve well to express the meaning of ministry as many lay persons have experienced it since Vatican II.

It can also express the contrasting experiences of lay-clergy and world-church relations. Insofar as care of society describes the liberative effect of ministry, it applies equally to ministry carried out by laity or clergy (both of whom are responsible for the care of society). What makes any act pastoral is not that a pastor does it but that it is done with the shepherding, freeing quality of Jesus. This quality should characterize the activity of all Christians.

Such an inclusive perspective will not rewrite history, but it can restore the biblical sense of equality among all the initiated, and it can reaffirm the contemporary sense of initiative and creativity especially felt among the laity. Being aware of the overriding meaning of shepherding can help everyone who looks at Christian history to see the way that meaning can get sidetracked. This awareness may prevent history from being repeated through us.

The symbol of the care of society can also advance the sense of freedom which theological approaches to lay-clergy relations endorse. These approaches encourage really new configurations of the tradition; they urge against predetermining how else the tradition may be understood, shaped, and enacted. The care of society is one attempt to do that very thing. Shepherding is as ancient as Christianity itself, but what else it might mean when connected first of all with society is an experience which is relatively new—or at least it shouldn't be predetermined by other uses of shepherding in the past.

Ultimately, the value of any symbol is its praxis. Here the care of society looks to the laity for practical experience and enactment. What the role of the ordained is and how the many internal church activities are viewed when interpreted from this perspective can only be determined by putting the care of society into practice deliberately and consistently. Whatever it holds, the symbol yearns to be concretized in practice, which is another source of lay-clergy relations.

The care of society is almost a paraphrase of world-church relations. The new spirit of Vatican II toward the world, the importance of the secularity of the laity, and the gradual secularizing of the clergy all find a congenial context in the notion of the care of society.

This chapter is an argument for the aptness of the symbol, the care of society, to interpret lay experience. It is one theologian's musing, reflecting a theologian's perception of what the experience of the laity is. Obviously, it is for the laity finally to decide that, and to interpret their own experience. If the care of society is apt, if it does symbolize appropriately what is going on, there should be some concrete implications, some new possibilities for understanding and action. The next chapter describes what those are.

# CHAPTER FIVE

## *Enactment*

SYMBOLS yearn for enactment. A good symbol opens up possibilities for new experience which are hard to resist. But to enact the possibilities disclosed by a symbol involves a transition from the realm of idea to the realm of action. Making the transition can be challenging and exciting. It is also difficult.

In order to enact any symbol, questions such as the following must be answered: What would happen if we acted out the symbol? How would that feel? Who would benefit? What would the benefits be? What would it take to achieve the benefits? How shall we proceed? Shall we do it? The questions become increasingly specific and practical and may even call for some degree of planning. They certainly call for anticipation.

Each enactment is a new experience which in turn may be reflected upon, symbolized, and enacted anew. After a while, this process yields a rich fund of experiences for living. It integrates theological/faith reflection with experience in a way that keeps both in balance. When this happens, theology becomes more relevant because it is related more integrally to our actual experience. And our experience becomes more meaningful because it is partly constituted by our theology.

The actual enactment of a symbol like the care of society cannot be done in a book. But it is possible to give some description of what the enactment of this symbol might look like if it were carried out. That is the purpose of this chapter. It is a "what if" piece of projection. What if lay persons enacted the care of society in this way? What would it take? What impact would it have on their spirituality, their drive for community? What if lay people began living like this? What if they already are? The projection is always an invitation: Does this seem feasible? attractive? consistent? Is it happening? Where? How? What's the experience? Let's hear about it, share it, live it. This final chapter will succeed if it is the beginning chapter of a dialogue on these very questions.

In order to concretize this projection somewhat, I want to introduce Anne and Jim. They are composite Catholic lay persons who embody the experience of many others. Through them I want to sketch what it means practically to care for society.

Jim and Anne are in their late 30s. They have been married for fifteen years and have three children. They were both raised in Catholic families and went to Catholic schools. They have childhood memories of the Catholic church before Vatican II, but for most of their adolescent and adult life Anne and Jim have known the postconciliar church.

Jim and Anne like the changes since Vatican II, even if sometimes they miss the feeling of security and order in the church they remember from their childhood. They welcome the opportunities for more active participation in liturgy, religious education, and parish life. They value the chance to express their views through parish committees and organizations. They appreciate the efforts of the priests and sisters who try to make the parish more like a community, and they prefer the friendly adult relationship they have with several priests to the formal, distant respect which they have for other priests. But most of all, they feel good about a new identity which is emerging for themselves.

Over the last few years both Anne and Jim have been gaining a new sense of their identities and roles as Christians. It has been a gradual process and many experiences have contributed to it. Raising their children has been a big influence. The decisions they have made about where to live, where to work, how to invest, when to have children, what kind of security to provide, the answers they've given to the children's questions, the values and behavior they have tried to instill—all these moments fed into their growing self-awareness. Similarly, relationships with family, relatives, friends, work associates, neighbors have constantly challenged them and given them opportunities to reflect on themselves, to test themselves, to create themselves.

There have been thousands of small contributions. A comment, a homily, an article in a magazine, a movie or TV show, an appeal from somebody's favorite cause, a vacation, Christmas, dieting, a family retreat, schoolwork, voting, anniversaries, a new hobby, questions. In ways forgotten and ways never known, Jim and Anne have become who they are. They can't articulate it very clearly or coherently, but they feel it.

What they feel is basically the freedom and the responsibility to live their lives as Christians in their world. They don't feel isolated or autonomous in doing so, but neither do they feel dependent on others to figure out what they need and to provide it for them. If Anne and Jim were to sum up their feeling in one word, it would be maturity. They feel mature in their faith and ready to live it as adult believers.

They don't necessarily think of themselves as ministers, but they do think of themselves as following Jesus, as using the gifts God has given them, as contributing what they can to make the world they live in better. The organized church is certainly important to them, but if they were to state it most accurately, they now feel that the church belongs to them more than they belong to the church. The church is at their service, just as they are at the service of the world—and for the same reason. Because that is the way God wants it. What does it mean, what does it take to be at the service of the world, to care for society as Jim and Anne live in it? It means four things.

### Love of the World

Anne and Jim love the world. They are at home in it. They can remember when they were children at school being warned about the temptations of worldly life, and there seemed to be a lot of anxiety about sex. But they never got the impression that the world was really evil or that enjoying its natural beauty and working to have a decent share of creature comforts was wrong. In fact, their memories of family, home, neighborhood strongly reinforced the idea that the world is good and it's good to be part of it. The same impression was conveyed through their parish churches which were full of colors, smells, objects, sounds, people.

This basic experience matured as they did. They learned about the world of nature, how it works, and how it must be cared for if we are to continue to enjoy it. The same was true of society, although it was often more difficult to feel the same way about unsightly factories and dumps, polluting plants, profit-only business interests, manipulative advertising and marketing practices, government waste and dishonesty, and so on. But these negative aspects did not overshadow their fundamental appreciation for the goodness of things, as found in nature or as made in society.

What has matured for Jim and Anne is their instinctive love for the world which has been reinforced and deepened as they have become better acquainted with God's love for the world. The turning point for them came one Christmas after their first child was born. The homily at Christmas Mass was pretty familiar. It stated simply and directly how God's love for us, for human life, for creation itself was manifested in the birth of Jesus. But for Anne and Jim, holding their two month old son, the words went deeper. They *felt* God's love in their own child, in their own love, in their basic, repeatable human experience. God loves the world, not just the world of nature, but the world of human beings, the societal world. For Jim and Anne this is the central truth and their lives pivot around it.

To believe in the incarnation of God in Jesus means for Anne and Jim that the world is worth it, as far as God is concerned. The birth of Jesus means they don't have to leave the world, society, home, work, neighborhood in order to find God. If the world is good enough for God, it surely is good enough for Jim and Anne. This fundamental conviction has been repeatedly reinforced for them by the world-affirming attitude that has generally characterized the post-Vatican II church which makes them feel even more at home.

This is not to say that the world is perfect or that finding God in the midst of schedules, taxes, business deals, personal conflicts, poverty, etc., is easy. But it does mean that the world itself, the actual experiences which make up the life that Anne and Jim share, is the chief *source* of their experience of God's love; it is *where* they encounter their living Lord; it is *how* their own incarnation of God's love takes place. And that has been the most significant realization for both of them. What happened in Jesus continues to happen in Jim and Anne. The love God has for their world, for their society is expressed through them.

They have even dared to think at times that their love of God can be real and present, in their world at least, only to the extent that they manifest it. And they can only manifest it to the extent that they own it, allow it to fill their hearts and be concretized in their care for the world around them. Anne and Jim have seen more and more clearly that to be Christian is to become God's love for the world as that love was shown in Jesus. Their own insight into that love can be expressed as follows.

God believes in society. Anne and Jim don't remember when they first heard this expression, but they do remember when they first confronted its meaning. Jim had just opened a restaurant after several years of managing restaurants for other people. Anne was doing part-time remedial teaching of children in a poor section of their city. As she got to know the families of the children, she became aware that several of their fathers, brothers, or other relatives were ex-offenders. Generally they had been imprisoned for armed robbery or selling stolen goods. Most of them had previous records, limited schooling, and no work experience.

Anne became particularly close to one family and discovered that the father could be paroled from prison if he had a job. She suggested to Jim that he hire the man to work in his restaurant. They both had mixed feelings about it. Their own stereotypes about criminals, the already risky venture of opening a restaurant, the reactions of their financial backers if something should go wrong, their desire to help others, their basic ambiguity about the values involved and how far they were willing to go to put those values into practice.

As long as they considered the situation from a business point of view, they were inclined not to take the risk. But whenever they viewed it from a faith point of view, they felt differently. Their earlier experience of God's love for the world, manifested to them in their first child, was very real and very influential. They began to ask themselves what God's love for the world means in *their* situation. How would their decision either incarnate or frustrate God's love?

They discussed this with a few friends, including one priest and the sister who first got Anne involved with remedial teaching. They spent time in quiet prayer and then, with no clear assurance, they decided to hire the ex-offender. What finally prompted their decision was the conviction that God believes in the world, in the power of opening up new possibilities for people, in the gift of freeing social systems to allow others to live their lives more fully.

The risks were not minimized because Jim and Anne acted out of their faith convictions, but then the risks were never minimized for God either. Anne and Jim soon discovered that their decision was opening up for them a new way to experience God and to deepen their relationship with God. They were reliving the divine experience; they were investing themselves as God had; they were caring for society.

In doing so, they began to pay closer attention to how God cares for society. God takes what society gives and transforms it, uses it to open up new possibilities for the future. God does not abandon society; God does not destroy society; God does not intervene and take over for society. God *works* with society. All of it, the good and the bad, the creative and the repetitive, the exciting and the boring, the energizing and the wearying, the life giving and the death bringing.

This is what Jesus' death-resurrection manifests so sharply. In one sense, the accumulation of forces that led to Jesus' death was the worst that human society could do. God did not prevent that act and God did not break the covenant because of it. Instead, God took the death of Jesus and transformed it into new life, not just for Jesus but for all of us, especially maybe for those who were actually involved in putting Jesus to death. That's how God works.

But it may be misleading to say simply "God works" or "God does such and such" as if God were working apart from or alongside of us. In all likelihood God was able to transform Jesus' death into resurrection because Jesus himself believed so deeply in the covenant, in the commitment of God to society. Without Jesus' own cooperation, God may not have been able to do all that God wanted to do. Jim and Anne have come to see that the relationship between Jesus and God is not just a unique experience between two persons of the Trinity but is the pattern of God's relating to and believing in all of us.

They have come to see that whatever God does, God does through us, with us. And if we aren't willing to let God do much, not much will happen. If we choose to approach society with an indifferent, cynical, hostile, selfish attitude, that pretty much dictates what God can do, at least through us.

This realization has a twofold effect. On the one hand it draws Anne and Jim more deeply into the mystery of God's life with us because they feel their importance to God (whether it is judged important by others or not). At the same time they are gripped by a sense of responsibility for how they feel about society, what kind of spirit they bring to their lives, where they put their energies, what decisions they make. Sometimes the feeling of responsibility can be almost overwhelming and burdensome. When that happens, they try to reclaim the awareness of *God's* investment and belief in society, and they try to take delight in the part they play in God's care for society. On both counts, the organized church is very helpful by providing learning opportunities, liturgical experiences, and friends who feel as they do.

God's belief in society means for Jim and Anne that society has a future. That future is not just society's but God's as well. To speak of God having a future once seemed as strange to Anne and Jim as to speak of God believing in society. But as they grow in their appreciation of what the covenant means, of what the incarnation ratifies, they realize that God is truly invested in society, that God's commitment has some implications for God.

God is not indifferent about what happens in society. God's own life-with-us is affected. If God is really living with us, sharing our experiences, working through us, transforming what we give, then God must have some feeling for what happens. And God's feeling is not just in relation to the present, or the past, but also the future. God anticipates, envisions, looks forward to—just like the rest of us. No, more than the rest of us because God sees and feels the whole present, the whole past, the whole future.

And God *wants* the best future for society that is possible, given the way things have actually gone up to now. God's desire, even passion, for the future reinforces God's belief in society.

Jim and Anne found it difficult to think of God as having feelings and desiring a future because they had been taught that God was beyond such changing, creaturely experiences. But the more they became familiar with the way Scripture describes God and the more they pondered what it means that God has *become* human in Jesus, the more comfortable they feel with a God who cares so deeply. God has not become less divine to them. In fact, God has become more divine in their view because they realize that to be so involved with human beings and not to quit, to get discouraged, to grow weary has to require a God. God's fidelity and passion and belief in them and love for the world have become more significant divine attributes for Anne and Jim than the attributes they learned as children.

All this was especially important for them when the ex-offender they hired began showing up late after a few weeks on the job and started quarreling with other employees. The first reaction of Jim and Anne was that this man didn't really want a job, that he didn't appreciate the chance he was being given. When they heard themselves say those things, it sounded very self-righteous. They began to suspect that the problem may have been more with them than with the ex-offender.

They tried putting themselves in his position. He was not used to working. He didn't know what it would take to get up every workday, be on time, do his job. He had spent the previous five years in a prison with nothing to do except regular kitchen duty. He was making $4.50 an hour, but a lot of his buddies were hustling for $4,000 a week. In short, Anne and Jim realized that it would take more than a job if this man were to have a real future.

And so, they faced another decision. How far should their investment in this one ex-offender go? How much could they be expected to do for him and how much could they expect him to do for himself? There were no easy answers to these questions, but Jim and Anne realized that whatever they did for others, however they tried to impact their world, they had to anticipate better than they had what else would be required if their efforts were to have a positive future. They couldn't know everything ahead of time, of course, but they had to let the future enter into their plans and decisions in the present.

They had a chance to test this when they decided to open a catering service out of the restaurant. They both felt they were now committed to working with ex-offenders. They knew they would need to hire drivers, arrangers, and servers. They even envisioned the possibility of the entire catering end of the business being run by ex-offenders. It seemed foolish, but Anne and Jim realized that if they were to care for society as God cares for society, it meant they believed in the future of society, not a future of dependence and a system of control, but a future of freedom and a system of creativity.

God's belief in society and commitment to its future carries a price. And God has been willing to pay that price. It is the price of disappointment, misunderstanding, blaming, even rejection. In staking the future of society on a cooperative venture *with us,* God is frequently disappointed in our meager response or our refusal to care for society as we should. In addition, God's way of working with us is often misunderstood. God is responsive to what we give, persuasive in offering us new initiatives for the future, but God does not intervene or coerce or usurp our role. Sometimes people expect God to take over, to punish those who misuse society, to prevent injustices from occurring, to protect us from all harm.

When God doesn't do this, some conclude God doesn't care while others blame God for not doing what *they* expect God to do. Ultimately, these misunderstandings can lead to a rejection of God, a disregard of divine enlightenment and strength in caring for society, or a claim that God doesn't even exist.

Any of the reactions just mentioned would be a high price for God to pay. At one time in their lives it never seriously occurred to Jim and Anne that God could actually be touched by our human rejection. *We* might eventually have to pay for it, but not God. Now they see it differently. Because God is so involved, so incarnated with us, our misunderstanding and rejection has to hurt, has to challenge God to remain faithful, to pay the price of loving our world.

Anne and Jim have had to pay the price too. The catering service bombed out. Not because the ex-offenders who ran it didn't do their job but because they were ex-offenders. Once word got around that the caterers were ex-offenders, business dropped off. People said they didn't want armed robbers standing around their living rooms or offices (presumably casing the place for a later break-in). It didn't matter that each employee was bonded or that the service was highly rated by former customers. Fears, stereotypes, competition, misunderstandings were too powerful. Jim and Anne's care of society was rejected.

So were they. One of the employees, when told that the catering service was going to fold, became so angry that he kept one of the delivery trucks overnight, went out drinking with some buddies (who were sure to say, "I told you so"), and ended up smashing the truck and damaging two other vehicles. Anne and Jim were liable. Their insurance just barely covered the expenses, but their premium tripled the following year. It was a very discouraging time.

But Jim and Anne had gained some facility in looking at situations through the experience of those whom society as a whole does not care for. They saw their former employee more as a victim than a victimizer of society. They knew he didn't belong back in jail; they knew they had to be faithful to the care of society.

What Anne and Jim did was to bid for the cafeteria service in two local high schools. They won the bid for one of them, transferred their catering service to a cafeteria service, staffed it with ex-offenders, and got their former employee back on a job-training program. Slowly, after the ex-offenders were in the school for a few months, they began to strike up friendships with some of the students. They'd talk about drugs, crime, education, racism, poverty. Word got to school officials.

Fortunately, the student counselors and principal saw this as an opportunity to benefit the students. They encouraged the rapping, stayed in touch with students and employees, worked out some agreements with Jim and Anne, and eventually hired one of the cafeteria workers as an assistant football coach. This time, the commitment was successful, beyond what Anne and Jim could have hoped for. And that led them to another insight into God's care for society.

As Jim and Anne thought about it, they realized that when God's care for society was successful, it was celebrated. A special meal, free time from work, building a memorial, symbolic activity. The achievement didn't have to be great or revolutionary. It just had to be real, concrete, experienced. Biblical people seemed to realize that their care for society was linked up with a celebration of thanks and praise of God. If God believes in society, stakes the future on it, pays the price for it, then God should be celebrated in the achievements of society too.

Anne and Jim have come to appreciate the value of "celebrating every success" as they call it. They had a special celebration when their first ex-offender got his initial paycheck. After the restaurant closed for the night, there was a gathering of the employees, the man's family, his parole officer, the sister who first introduced the family to Anne, and other friends. There were no speeches, no formal prayers, no excessive celebrating. Just a moment to let the meaning of the event and the feelings it generated be shared.

Jim has come to see his restuarant business as a kind of societal feeding, for which he at least gives thanks and over which he presides. Anne has interpreted her teaching as a kind of liturgy of the word, where she teaches what others have said and helps each student proclaim their own message. Worship on Sunday has had a richer meaning for Jim and Anne since they began to care for society so consciously. The point for both of them is not to pat themselves on the back or to make more out of daily events than is really there. The point is to join in and increase the delight of the Lord.

That is the crowning achievement of Anne and Jim's growing love of the world. It is a deepening relationship with the God who cares for society. In their own care, Jim and Anne share the divine experience more fully and want to invest themselves in the society they inhabit more deeply.

This first practical implication of enacting the care of society corresponds to the first issue, cited in chapter one, of the value of ministry in the world. As presented there, the question is whether ministry in the world will be considered just as important as ministry in the church. The two are usually in tension. This can be a healthy tension, but it can also be divisive and weakening. There is need for both and lay persons are qualified to do both.

The care of society attempts to keep both together by drawing upon the rich tradition of pastoral care in the church and by drawing on the equally rich experience of Christians who live in and love the world. Each informs the other. Anne and Jim can interpret their feeling-for the world in faith terms because the church has preserved and developed a full account of the meaning of care which they can tap into. At the same time, Jim and Anne can add to that account by their own experience of care in society.

The wholeness, the integrity of each calls for the other. One should not be spoken of or undertaken without the other. Granted, this is only a conceptual wholeness as described here. What happens in practice is always another story. But the potential of a symbol like the care of society is that it includes both poles of ministry; it is a constant reminder of the mutuality of church ministry and world ministry, of the contributions each can make to the other. A symbol can do no more than open the way to enactment.

If the work of pastoral care retains its societal orientation and if the work of caring for society retains its pastoral dimension, then the relative importance, even equality, of each can be better maintained. Then too the primary question will be, not who is working where (clergy-church; laity-world), but how well is the total ministry being carried out. It would even seem, if the connection and mutuality is essential, that some clergy should work in society and some laity should work in the church to reaffirm that there is not a separation but a synthesis and that each form of service belongs in the other arena.

## Lay Authority

When Anne and Jim were growing up, the most important value in their religious experience was obedience. They learned from their parents, from their teachers in school, from priests, and from other now-forgotten sources that the best way to please God was to follow the direction given by those in authority in the church.

That attitude began to change for Jim and Anne as they matured. Part of the change was the normal growing-up process, but part of it was the change in the church itself. Just as they were becoming young adults, church authorities began stressing how each person must take responsibility for his or her faith and really choose to live as a Christian, and as a Catholic. Anne and Jim struggled with the implications of that challenge as did their peers.

Many chose to leave the church, claiming it had all been kind of childish and silly anyway. Many stopped doing what they used to do but stayed in fairly regular contact with the church. Some got really turned on to the possibilities for a new church and became more involved than ever.

Jim and Anne followed a mixed pattern. Some things they rejected; some things they continued; and some things they felt really excited about. They went through periods of not going to church, of questioning certain teachings (especially regarding birth control, the divinity of Jesus, the meaning of the sacraments), of testing their own freedom to make decisions about their faith life and to act accordingly. The old emphasis on obedience and the old feelings of security sometimes seemed very appealing. Most of the time, though, they seemed like pieces of a past which was not going to return. To go back, or stay back, in those days would be wrong. But what the new age held they didn't see clearly.

In this regard, Anne and Jim were very good for each other. They first met in college through some campus ministry activities. They discovered a mutual concern for the church, or rather their relationship to the church. They had both been raised in a strong Catholic environment, had many of the same experiences, and felt uncertain about what it meant to be a Catholic anymore.

As they talked about these things and participated in different activities, their friendship grew. They were clearly believers, two people who cared about their spiritual lives and how to live them in a changing church and a turbulent society. They became each other's best sounding board and guide. They found that their faith and their life was more exciting and more stimulating when they were together. A year after graduation, they decided to marry.

Their marriage provided them with two pivotal experiences. One was the opportunity to plan their wedding liturgy; the other was the responsibility to plan their family. In both instances, they experienced themselves being in charge of their own lives. It was exciting and a little scary at the same time. They had ample assistance from church professionals in making their decision in both areas, but they knew that the final choices were theirs, and they claimed that authority. They made their choices carefully, respectfully, conscientiously, freely.

That was the beginning of a pattern in their lives that might be called lay authority. It is an essential ingredient in the care of society. Lay authority refers to the special competence of lay persons to make the decisions that shape their lives and incarnate God's love in *their* world. Because their world is so intimately bound up with society itself, lay authority is intrinsic to the care of society.

Lay authority derives from the very positions in society which lay persons hold. These positions are where God is. Lay persons enter a society that is already filled with God's presence, God's power, God's wisdom, God's love. Lay authority is the gift which God offers to believers which enables them to tap into that divine presence and to act on it, to act out of it.

In this sense, lay authority does not originate somewhere else (in heaven, in the organized church, in the clergy) and then get transferred to society. It is already in society because God is already in society. However, the exercise of lay authority in the concrete occasions which constitute society is not totally independent of the authority which is invested in the church and its office holders. Just as with pastoral care and the care of society, there is a relationship between lay authority and official church authority. At its fullest, that relationship recognizes and expresses the authenticity, complementarity, and stewardship of both lay and official church authority. It also transcends the discussion of the power of orders and the power of jurisdiction (as noted in the introduction and also in chapter three). The classic issue of powers is part of a one-sided identification of power and authority within the organized church.

What is envisioned here is a different frame of reference which seeks the complementary relationship of authority, vested in various ways among the whole People of God.

In the past, this relationship was more monolithic than mutual. Official church authority clarified the principles and values and general program thrust of social action, and the laity put it into practice. The assumption behind this was not that the laity didn't know what to do unless they were told but rather that what the official church taught was presumed to be what the laity believed, or would spontaneously assent to once it was articulated (hence, John Henry Newman's advice that the hierarchy consult the faithful, as noted in the introduction). Moreover, what the laity put into practice was presumed to be what the official church meant by their teaching (hence, John Henry Newman's other claim that doctrine develops as the whole church lives out the meaning of God's truth).

The same assumption governs lay authority in the care of society. The difference is that the clear distinction between the church's office holders who do the teaching and the laity who do the enacting is replaced by a holistic, integral appreciation of the mutual teaching and enacting of all the members of the church. If there are special, distinctive competencies to be identified, this is done on the basis of the specific issue, not on the basis of whether a person belongs to the clergy or the laity.

Ordinarily, the clergy are primarily involved in the organized church life and therefore are presumed to have the competence and authority which are required to care for the church. Similarly, the laity are primarily involved in societal life and therefore are presumed to have the competence and authority which are required to care for society. The distinction is not an absolute, of course. Lay persons who are more deeply involved in organized church life (especially church professionals and volunteers) may be presumed to have the same type of competence and authority as the clergy. Likewise, clergy who are more deeply involved in societal life may be presumed to have the same type of competence and authority as the laity.

The point is that the concrete circumstances in which Christian life is carried out are the source of authority. Distinctions between clergy and laity, between official church authority and lay authority are useful only insofar as they point to the concrete circumstances in which a particular event is being lived out. In that case, it isn't clergy as such or laity as such but rather internal church life symbolized by clergy or the care of society symbolized by laity which is the decisive point. The authority of one is never isolated or alienated from the other, although each is relatively autonomous from the other.

They are *relatively* autonomous because there is only one ultimate source of authority for Christians and that is the Holy Spirit. The one Spirit gifts persons appropriately so they may fulfill their potential (for ministry, for care) where they are. Different settings yield different gifts, but all are relative to each other or interdependent with each other. This is the variety and diversity which has been re-emphasized in the church since Vatican II.

At the same time, lay authority is relatively *autonomous* from official church authority (and vice versa), because the primary source of both the teaching and acting in society is the setting where the Holy Spirit is actually working. In terms of the care of society, the setting for the Spirit's work is society. The Spirit's movement there is not opposed to the Spirit's movement in the church, but it is different. And those in the best position to know this and act on it are the laity.

It took Jim and Anne a long time to acknowledge this and to feel free enough to act on it. They are still growing in their sense of authority and each experience in which they exercise it helps. Their restaurant business has provided endless occasions for the exercise of such authority: where to locate the restaurant, whose financial backing to seek, whom to hire and what to pay employees, what to charge customers, where to get supplies, how to handle competition, what sort of advertising to use, whether to join various civic clubs and organizations, what to do with the profits (when there were some). All these are basic business questions, but for Anne and Jim, they are also faith questions. Every one of them touches on some aspect of justice and makes a statement about their values. In addition, Jim and Anne see their business as a service of hospitality to others, providing a pleasing atmosphere and experience which may actually be healing or refreshing to some customers. And they struggle with questions about wasted food, theft, excessive drinking, and even working on Sunday.

The same kinds of questions arose when Anne wanted to teach again. Where to teach? Who would benefit? What were the risks, the commitments? How did the family figure in?

When facing these and many other societal situations, Anne and Jim want to look at *all* the resources available to them through the church. They have reflected on official teachings and theological commentaries/opinions; they have consulted; they have prayed. Jim and Anne never felt obliged to follow exactly any of the input they received.

They realized that no one else was precisely in their position and that they were responsible for their decisions.

As Anne and Jim have grown in their own sense of lay authority, they have been gratified to find many clergy who are encouraging and supportive of their freedom to make responsible decisions. And they have also encountered others who seem to operate out of a presumption that the clergy have all the authority and the laity depend on them for guidance.

Jim and Anne experienced both reactions when their employees wanted to unionize. They reviewed the church's official teachings about trade unions and found a supportive, encouraging attitude among those they consulted. Yet, they also realized that none of the employees in their parish were unionized and very few employees in other parishes or the diocese were unionized. When Anne and Jim raised this question, they were curtly informed either that the situations were different or that the unionization of church personnel was being investigated.

Jim and Anne know that they are living through a time of transition in the church and old attitudes will still be encountered. Nonetheless, it disturbs them to be treated as less than adult or to be viewed as a threat. They have also occasionally been disappointed by those who are verbally affirmative of the laity but pull back when it is time for action.

This came home to them forcefully when Anne proposed a remedial education program through their parish school. She had been working in a successful program for two years and was always encouraged and affirmed by the parish priest. But when she broached the idea of using the parish school for a similar program and attracting children from nearby, but less proficient schools, she heard only about the problems involved (which she knew well and had dealt with already). The encouragement and affirmation didn't get transferred when the proposal involved action within and by the parish.

As Anne and Jim have been trying to grasp more deeply the meaning of their experience of lay authority, they have come across a traditional term—the sense of the faithful. They never did know exactly what it meant, but they associated it with the idea that the laity assent to what the hierarchy teaches. Now they see in that term an expression of their own feeling that their experience is a *source* of the church's understanding; that their actions are a source of the church's practice. It can come *from* them as well as come *to* them.

This is the area where Jim and Anne feel least satisfied. After receiving input and support from the church (clergy and laity alike) and making their own decisions, they don't always know how to channel their experience back into the church. They sometimes feel isolated at precisely the point they want to be most in touch with others—sharing the results of their care of society.

This desire ties in with their general feeling that the church belongs to them, that they are the church. Not by themselves, of course. They are the church only with everyone else who is the church. This includes the clergy as well as laity who are not in their particular situation or who are not facing their specific issues. All the People of God constitute the church, but Anne and Jim used to feel the clergy were somehow more the church than they were, largely because the clergy had the authority, the training and calling, the role, the status to represent the whole church.

Jim and Anne can still affirm that representative role as long as they think of the church as it organizes its own life and represents itself to itself. But this is only one side of the church and, they now believe, not its primary side. The church exists for the sake of others. It has a mission to reach out and care for the society it inhabits. In this context, it is the laity who are primary, who are more the church than the clergy (if such a comparison is to be made) because they have the authority, the experience and calling, the role, the status that makes them the church in society (which is a little different from being an ecclesial presence to the world, as described in Leonard Doohan's second model).

This view has helped Anne and Jim see themselves in a new way, feel themselves as the primary carers of Christ's church in society, claim their gifts and authority, and exercise them. This view has helped also to see the clergy differently. Jim and Anne value the clergy's contributions within the church, but they also acknowledge the limitation of the clergy's contribution to their own work. Rather than flaunt their new-felt autonomy, Anne and Jim long to reciprocate, to share their experience more fully with all the faithful, to become in practice the church they claim to be in principle.

Their sense of authority is moving Jim and Anne to want to contribute to the church the experience they have to give. They are bold enough to think that their care of society is valuable enough to contribute to the church's general interpretation and teaching in related areas. They have learned so much from their experience that they want to feed that into the church just as they want to be fed by what has been learned from the experiences of others. For a while Anne and Jim kept waiting for someone else to meet their needs. Then they realized that part of their authority means meeting their own needs, or at least initiating a process for meeting them. This has been especially evident in the areas of spirituality and community, which will be discussed next.

The emergence of lay authority touches on the second major issue cited in chapter one—the role of the clergy. As described there, the question was whether the clergy are ready for a laity which feels its own authority, values its own experience, and helps create the church by its actions and decisions.

In that regard the term shared responsibility was used. The term is applicable here if what is shared is a recognition of the authority to fulfill the responsibilities pertinent to each one's situation. Such recognition does not mean a hands-off, independent isolation from each other. It means each is a primary consultant to the other and stands ready to advise, support, and share the result of the other's experience.

Part of the implication of this presentation is that there are two relatively autonomous spheres of Christian activity which generate two relatively autonomous exercises of authority. The key to holding the two together is in acknowledging the one source of all authority and learning to accept the limits to authority that come with one's own particular setting.

If the latter were done, two things would result. The issue of authority would give rise to a *spiritual* interest because the focus would not be on who has what authority over whom but how is all authority actually manifesting the Spirit. This leads to the second result. If we all acknowledged the Spirit in our authority decisions, we would acknowledge that we don't *know* how the Spirit is working unless we listen to each other tell the stories from our personal experience.

### Spirituality of Engagement

When Anne and Jim think about the spirituality of their childhood, they recall that it wasn't called spirituality. The emphasis was on being a good Catholic. This meant practicing the faith by weekly attendance at Sunday Mass, monthly confession, frequent public devotions (novenas, benediction, way of the cross) and regular family devotions (rosary, night and meal prayers). Prayer was either led by someone else or it followed set formulas or was completely private. The spiritual life seemed like a great, mysterious other world that Jim and Anne had to enter into. It did not come from within them, and it did not always express what they were actually feeling.

As they grew older, it expressed even less what they were feeling. But fortunately for them, just at that time the Catholic practice of prayer and spirituality began to change. More spontaneity and informality were encouraged. The liturgy was celebrated in English and had opportunities for active participation through song, responses, and petitions. Anne and Jim attended several events (like a Cursillo and a Marriage Encounter) which were built around the idea of people sharing with one another their faith experiences, their questions, their own way of expressing prayer.

Jim and Anne found all this encouraging and helpful. But they still had the feeling that their prayer life was too separated from the rest of their lives. They learned how to use their own words to pray and they felt comfortable including their concerns and friends in common prayers, but Anne and Jim still felt they were plugging into something outside of themselves. The closest they could get to a different experience was when they could celebrate the sacrament of reconciliation jointly with a priest who seemed to appreciate the importance of their life together. On those occasions, they felt like their life experience was giving rise to their prayer experience. That felt integral.

But on the whole, Jim and Anne kept looking for a stimulus to nurture the spirit of their daily life. They tried reading spiritual masters or adaptations of the great spiritual writers, but this didn't really feel congruent with their experience. It was as if, once again, they had to "get into" the world of this literature in order to nurture their spiritual life. Anne and Jim wanted something more integral, more imbedded in their own experience. It began to occur to them that they might have to create it themselves.

At first, Jim and Anne shied away from such a thought. It sounded arrogant to say that the great spiritual tradition of the church wasn't good enough for them, that it didn't meet their needs, or that they were even capable of creating a spirituality for themselves. They recognized in this the persistence of their childhood training with its overemphasis on conformity and obedience and fitting in to what the church offers. But they also realized that they were not talking about a completely new, independent kind of spirituality. They were talking about claiming their own authority as adult believers and drawing from the church that belongs to them the resources for a spiritual life which they could give back to the church—because they also belong to the church.

The turning point came for Anne and Jim one weekend when they decided to drive a man and his two children to visit his wife who was in a women's federal prison. The prison was over ninety miles away and no public transportation went to the small town where it was located. As a result, most of the women were visited by their families rarely, if ever. Jim had found out about this situation when he casually asked the husband, who was working for him in the restaurant, about his plans for the weekend. The man explained that he'd like to visit his wife (who was in prison for writing bad checks) but that he had no way of getting there.

As Jim went home that night, thinking of his weekend plans with his family, he could not get the man's helpless, frustrated appearance out of his mind. He and Anne talked about it and decided to drive him and his two children to the prison. The trip took almost three hours because the route was very hilly with narrow roads. Conversation along the way was strained. They didn't have that much to talk about, and since they had never traveled here before they were all a little tense about the trip.

When they finally arrived, only one hour was left for visiting. When the hour was up, they turned around and headed back because there was nowhere to eat in the town. On the way back, Anne was able to elicit a little more conversation from the man and his children. They talked simply and honestly about their feelings, their loss and embarrassment, their anger at the location and treatment of the women, their gratitude for their chance to visit.

As he listened to the conversation Jim decided to stop at a restaurant so everyone could eat. Their meal was highlighted when the husband asked if he could say grace. Spontaneously and sincerely, he thanked the Lord for the blessings of this day and for Jim and Anne. After taking them home, Anne and Jim reflected on the experience. Jim said he thought Anne had been marvelous getting them to talk on the way home from the prison. Listening to them was like hearing a gospel parable. Anne said she thought of Jim as celebrating a eucharistic meal with them when they sat down to dinner. They listened to each other carefully;

they tried to understand the full meaning of what they were saying. Jim and Anne did not go to Mass the next day. They felt they had already celebrated the meaning of eucharist at a very deep and real level. Their care for society had given them the authority to enact their spiritual life as fully as it could be done on this particular occasion.

Once Anne and Jim began to look to their own experience for the source of their spiritual life, they could identify occasions when they felt most alive, most fulfilled, most in touch with the Lord. Such experiences held for them the clue to an integrated, holistic spirituality. The more they thought about it, the more they found themselves using three words: encounter, engagement, freedom.

Encounter means contact; engagement means entering in, becoming part of, relating, affecting and being affected; freedom means losing something of themselves while gaining something of another. Througn it all, there is a feeling that this occasion, this experience is real; it is definite; it is actual; it is unrepeatable; it is something where previously there was nothing.

These experiences fed their enthusiasm for a spirituality of engagement. Jim and Anne began to pay more attention to experiences which engaged them, drew them in more completely, summoned more from them. The encounters which had this effect most often were also encounters which constituted their family life, work, and general activities in society.

Anne and Jim felt they had identified the *source* of their spirituality, but they weren't sure what to do with it. They knew that making a business decision or organizing a meeting or teaching someone to read better or spending a weekend with the kids in the woods did not automatically mean they had prayed or encountered the Lord or deepened their union with the Spirit. Then another pivotal event occurred.

The week after their trip to the women's prison, Jim and Anne went to Sunday eucharist. The gospel that day was the story of Zaccheus and the homily accented the value of Christian hospitality. There were no further practical implications drawn out but Anne and Jim both felt like the story paralleled their recent experience.

They first identified with Zaccheus, who had resources and could offer them to someone who had none (Jesus). Like Zaccheus, they tended to stay at a distance, watching. When they were drawn in, engaged in the event, something very important, even decisive, happened. They assumed a new role, as Zaccheus had; they became a sign of God's care in society. It was as if the Zaccheus incident were being acted out anew, in their lives. It fit; it offered the congruence they were seeking. As they pondered the implications further, they felt that perhaps the better identification was not with Zaccheus but with Jesus.

Jim and Anne put themselves in Jesus' place and looked at Zaccheus. Why did Jesus take the initiative with Zaccheus? Why did Jim ask what his employee's plans for the weekend were? What did Zaccheus have to offer Jesus? What did a weekend ride to prison have to offer Jim and Anne? What did Jesus have to offer Zaccheus? What might happen if they really engaged each other? Could salvation come to both their houses that day?

This experience prompted Anne and Jim to begin connecting their life experiences more consistently with the stories recorded in Scripture. As they lived their story, they found parallels in the biblical stories. The more they oriented themselves in this way, the more they saw a kind of pattern opening up, starting with their engagement of life in society.

The first part of the pattern is sheer *expectation*. Jim and Anne have come to expect that their engagement in the care of society is the prime source of experiences where they meet the Lord. This expectation engenders an enthusiasm for the events and people which occupy so much of their time and energy. It keeps fresh the associations in their lives which otherwise might become routine and even burdensome. And most of all, it centers their spiritual life on the biblical accounts of engagement between the People of God and their Lord.

The accounts of biblical events, the stories of people just like Anne and Jim provide the framework for their expectation and enthusiasm. The biblical stories are reenacted in every age. Circumstances change, but the underlying experiences and the everpresent Lord endure. Jim and Anne have begun to see themselves as agents for reliving the Bible, for providing the Lord with opportunities to act out again the saving events of history.

The second part of the pattern flows from the first. The intersection of the biblical stories with Anne and Jim's stories is itself a new story. The new story, however, comes into existence as it is *communicated*. When Jim and Anne first made a connection between their care for the family and the Zaccheus incident, they wanted to share their new-found meaning. It was simple enough to do. They just got together the friends who had watched their children that day and told them how the story of Zaccheus seemed to interpret their own experience. During this conversation, it was actually the other couple who suggested that Anne and Jim might identify with Jesus rather than Zaccheus. Their comment opened up a new dimension for Jim and Anne, which occurred *in the communicating* of the stories.

Anne and Jim have continued to generate this kind of shared reflection although they have avoided setting up weekly discussions or regular groups or organizing anything very formal. They prefer to let their experience determine the pace and pattern of their sharing as well as who they communicate with. Here the parish is a great resource since it is a gathering of many similar persons who might otherwise be unknown to Jim and Anne. Of course, they also engage in this way others who are neighbors, work associates, friends in other churches.

Also, Anne and Jim are not the only ones to initiate such conversations. They are sometimes engaged by others, or they participate in church-sponsored discussion or encounter groups, or they plug into civic and ecumenical events which offer the same opportunity. Whatever the setting, whoever initiates it, Jim and Anne find that their spiritual life grows out of engagements with others in which they tell their own stories, relate them to the biblical stories, and catch new insights or stimuli which prompt them to keep integrating their care of society with the biblical stories of their faith.

In doing so, Anne and Jim have been led to study the Bible more closely, to read commentaries which put the biblical stories in their historical and literary context while highlighting their religious meaning. In a way, Jim and Anne go through a process similar to preparing a sermon or homily except that they start with their own story rather than a portion of God's story (as arranged in the lectionary for Sundays) and they usually sift through the meanings and connections with others rather than privately.

The input from others is especially enriching. It extends Anne and Jim's own thinking. Often images or themes are picked up which might not have occurred to them. Sometimes, just telling someone else their own thoughts has helped Jim and Anne to clarify their insights as they hear themselves explain them. Putting out ideas or feelings or hunches for others to respond to is a valuable exercise.

When Anne's first year of remedial teaching was coming to a close, she began to feel a real sense of loss because she had developed a personal friendship with several of the children and their families. As she described her feelings to two other teachers, it sounded to Anne like a lot of self-concern, if not self-pity. She didn't like that and didn't want it, but her anticipation of breaking off her relationships with these children was very distressing.

Anne was sharing this while the three of them were driving home after the last class. They were all feeling about the same, when the driver suddenly stopped the car. "This sounds silly," she said, "but do you know what I just thought of? Last Sunday's gospel. It was the story of the disciples on their way to Emmaus. Remember how sad they felt because they thought Jesus was dead?" Before she could draw out the parallels, Anne and the other teacher jumped in. They explored the connections all the way home and for the rest of the afternoon.

Their conclusion was that they had to share their experience, just as the disciples had. Eventually they arranged to speak briefly during the adult education hour on one Sunday about remedial teaching, hoping to attract other interested and qualified parishioners. They had two of the children and their families present as well. Only about fifteen parishioners showed up, but when they all went to Mass afterward they had a deeper sense of union with those first disciples.

The end result of engagement spirituality is to encounter the Lord who is already in the events which are engaged. The goal is not to get definite answers or better strategies or clearer objectives in caring for society. It is the experience of the Lord in the acts of caring. Focusing on one's own stories and relating them to the biblical stories opens up the experience of the Lord better and more consistently than anything else for Anne and Jim.

It is not just putting into accurate words an experience which is already known. It is a renewing and reliving of that experience in the act of sharing it. This type of communication often has the character of proclamation. Giving new expression to an experience renews the experience itself and provides a fresh feeling of it. This energizes the participants to keep experiencing the Lord in their caring for society. When the Lord emerges out of the experience, a spirituality of engagement is happening.

And when it happens, it yearns for *celebration*. This is the third aspect of a spirituality of engagement. Celebration is a relatively new term in Jim and Anne's spiritual vocabulary. They learned it as they learned a new way to worship publicly after Vatican II. Celebrating liturgy conveyed a quite different experience from "attending or going to Mass." As they matured in both their understanding and experience of liturgical celebration, they also realized that celebration is not only joyful, smiling, exuberant excitement. Anne and Jim can celebrate funerals and penance and crises as well as they can celebrate weddings and Easter. It isn't the mood so much as the meaning which makes an event a celebration.

And the richest meaning of celebration for them is to express what they feel as they care for society. What they feel grows out of each specific occasion in which they engage in caring activity. Sometimes the celebration is simple, spontaneous, and immediate, like the time when Anne and her two friends found themselves reenacting the Emmaus event. Sometimes the celebration may be more elaborate, planned, even postponed for a while, like the time Jim and Anne planned an awards night for the ex-offenders who had been working in their restaurant for one year.

These celebration moments have given Anne and Jim a new appreciation for the public liturgical celebrations of the church. The rituals offer a framework for inserting, privately or publicly, their own experiences and uniting them with the common prayer of the church. Occasionally, Jim and Anne have gotten involved in planning special liturgies at their parish (on Thanksgiving or Labor Day, for instance). More often, they lead what they call domestic liturgies—celebrations which express their experience of caring for society and which do so with the people who care with them.

Jim and Anne find that they often adapt or draw upon official church rituals for their domestic celebrations. Sometimes they are more innovative and create their own. Always they feel their spirituality integral with their life. Every experience reinforces their direction and unifies their lives and identities as believers whose care for society engages them in the life of their Lord.

The emergence of an engagement spirituality obviously addresses the third issue cited in chapter one—a lay spirituality. As described briefly in that context, such a spirituality would be integral to the life experience of lay persons—that means integral to life in society, to the engagement of believers in caring for society.

The spirituality outlined here takes the lay experience of caring for society as the *source* of spiritual growth. It expects to find the Lord in that experience through the stories which constitute life in society today. These daily stories are oriented to the biblical parallels. Reflecting on these parallels enables people to make connections which can then be communicated and celebrated.

This type of spirituality grows out of experience. It does not rely so much on set routines, daily prayer, or spiritual books. It takes spirituality as a quest, a discovery, a search. The outcome is not known ahead of time. Along the way, there is much to learn (or be reminded of), room for many points of view, opportunities for creativity and always for concrete action. Engagement spirituality focuses on biblical and liturgical resources for its nourishment, and it values all of life as actually lived to stimulate prayerful experience.

Engagement spirituality does something else. It leads to a new experience of community.

## Occasion-Centered Community

When Anne and Jim were growing up they didn't hear much about community. They knew they belonged to "the church" and had close ties with their parish. But they don't remember any other affiliation being singled out for special attention. As long as they were good, practicing Catholics, they fulfilled what was meant by belonging to the church.

But that didn't fulfill their own expectations as they grew older. They were part of a generation that looked critically at their institutions and traditions. They demanded more than compliance; they pushed for creativity and meaning. They wanted to find themselves and others at a deeper, more intimate level than they had experienced growing up. They joined in the search for community.

For a while social causes supplied this desire. They often said they experienced more community with a mixed group of peace protesters than they did with parishioners at Sunday Mass. They felt greater acceptance at times from eccentric street people or belligerent activists than from the priests or teachers or fellow believers who claimed to be their faith family.

Jim and Anne never lived in any communes, but a lot of their friends did. They visited often enough to have some idea what that experience was, but they never felt attracted to it for themselves. They were more attracted to each other and to the community they experienced with each other or could offer when they got their friends together. They felt caught between wanting community while not wanting to get stuck in expectations or habits that would become artificial, limiting, merely external to their innermost feelings.

One of the motives for marrying each other was their desire for community and their inability to find a satisfying experience of it with others. They began to envision their own community, a family that would be open to others, take initiatives, be supportive but not become overly structured or rely too much on habit. They found that it was not easy to strike the balance they wanted.

When they began having children, they realized how much of their lives were dictated by the children's needs. At first, they resisted "being controlled" in this way. Then they noticed the same pattern regarding work, extended family ties, church activities, social concerns, friendships. Their lives often seemed fragmented; they frequently felt like they were going in several directions at once. Community began to fade as an attainable goal.

Then they took a different point of view. It occurred when Anne and Jim held an awards night for the ex-offenders who had been working for a year in their restaurant. They invited everyone who was connected in any way with the success story of these three employees: their families, friends, co-workers, parole officers, social workers, customers, ministers. In all, over fifty people with all kinds of backgrounds assembled in the hall of the church where one of the employees was a member. There was much socializing and getting acquainted as people met each other for the first time and shared a few hours together.

The highlight came when Jim and Anne presented each of the three workers with a certificate of achievement. Each of them spoke briefly. One said he had never gotten a certificate or diploma of any kind before in his life. Another said there hadn't been this many people at his wedding and he felt *that* was his proudest moment. The third said he had learned to believe in himself because somebody else finally did. It was a powerful, unifying moment.

Afterward, Jim's restaurant manager was obviously moved by the whole event and suggested that they'd have to do it again next year. Later that night Jim mentioned the comment to Anne. He didn't know why but somehow he felt that this was a one-time occasion. There was no need to do it again, to perpetuate it annually. Next year might be something different, but this was enough. It was all it could have been. And that was enough; it was good.

Anne and Jim reflected on the experience and their feelings about what it meant, how they really had felt community that night, how it all came out of their small attempt to care for others and gather together everyone else who participated in that caring. They felt like they had created community on that occasion. Their instinct was not to continue that, but to create community on other occasions, to let occasions of caring for society be the source and the definition of the community experience they wanted.

In Jim and Anne's mind, this complemented the way they were developing their spirituality. They were assembling a spirituality out of individual, specific acts of caring for society. They were letting their experience lead them in spiritual growth. Why couldn't they do the same for community? Instead of conceiving community as a relatively stable environment in which people interact in expected ways to provide a reinforcing and secure experience, why not conceive of community as the experience of being-with people who care for society *in the occasions* of their caring.

Community is then centered around the events which constitute specific, limited acts of caring. The experience of being-with others within the event is community. It lasts as long as the occasion lasts. It may endure afterward in the memory, the story, the feeling that each one carries away, but there is no need to set up a schedule or pattern for repeating the event or the experience. In fact, that very tendency squelched more community feeling than anything else in Anne and Jim's experience.

In effect, they began to think of community as what happens during the actual occasions of caring for society. They realized that they have a lot to do with what happens, but they focused their attention more on each discrete event and less on how to perpetuate it or insure its repetition or proclaim to others what happened in a separate experience.

This view of community has felt right to Jim and Anne. It corresponds to the way they actually live their lives—in episodes, with people who for the duration of that occasion are intimately associated in the creation of an experience. Each occasion is new, fresh, with its own possibilities. Exploring the novelty of every occasion keeps Anne and Jim alive to what the *occasion* offers, which for them means how the Lord may be encountered and engaged this time. Experiencing that is ample community.

The need to build in continuation, to insure repetition has diminished for Jim and Anne because their experience tells them there are always opportunities for community as long as they care for society. Their experience also tells them that the richest experiences of community involve others outside their family, outside their acquaintances, outside the people they know and are comfortable with. Sometimes they have to push themselves to keep including others who are not well known to them, who are threatening or disagreeable, who have different views or background. That effort is a big part of their discipline, their asceticism, which bridges their spirituality and community.

An occasion-centered community experience is not always planned. Sometimes Anne and Jim find themselves drawn together with others while working on a common project and they never intended the occasion to generate a community experience. At other times they may set out to bring people together or use a planned occasion to feed their experience of community and nothing much happens.

The focus for them is the feeling, the quality, the experience of being together with others on *this* occasion to care for society.

Such a focus has given Jim and Anne a new appreciation of the efforts of the clergy to "build community" in parishes. They value these occasions too, but they do not consider them their primary experience of community. Rather, such gatherings enable Anne and Jim to sum up as a whole their numerous, individual experiences and to symbolize them in a new occasion which is explicitly grounded in their faith.

This type of occasion-centered community corresponds to the desire of many lay persons for community experience as noted at the end of chapter one. It grows out of the actual episodes which constitute daily life, and it prizes those events as the source of community. It is open to others and it remains free of overstructure. At the same time there is both a need and a value in being able to put together a series of individual occasions. Otherwise, life reverts to being a fragmented hodge-podge with no sense of wholeness or integrity.

This is where the church in its typical efforts to achieve community is helpful. In its stories, its symbols, its worship, its history, its future, its humanness, its transcendence, the church *is* an environment in which many people and many experiences can find room to reside. Because the church, in its divine dimension, preexists all of us, it offers a setting of wholeness, of stability, of presence that cannot be generated by ourselves alone.

Efforts to "build community" are ultimately efforts to awaken our sensitivity to this gift, to appreciate it and inhabit it more deeply. Whether this or that planned activity in the church comes off as well as hoped is not so important. What is important is that we can bring the occasions of our lives and let them play their part in filling in and concretizing the profound, already present community which our God offers us as a constant gift. When our own discrete occasions are permeated by that feeling and lifted into a larger whole, we know why the church is integral to our life and where we can find the Lord who cares for us.

The four aspects just discussed are required to enact the care of society. They constitute what might be called a laicizing of ministry. Ordinarily, laicizing has a negative connotation in the church. It means that an ordained person is "reduced to the lay state," the assumption being that to leave the hierarchy is to go lower (reflecting a hierarchical mind-set which is truly higher-archical).

Obviously, the term laicizing as used here does not have this connotation. In fact, it aims at saying just the opposite. Vatican II has helped to restore a holistic sense of the church as all the People of God who together share the one mission of Jesus. The laicizing of ministry means that the lay experience is taken as primary, as the first context or frame of reference for interpreting our common mission. As presented here, that mission is to care for society. This is what all ministry is primarily about; this is the responsibility of all Christians.

If other forms of care (ministry) are acceptable and desirable (such as those within the church), they are nonetheless viewed *in relation to* the care of society. If some members of the church (such as the ordained or church professionals) are designated for these other forms of ministry, they are viewed *in relation to* the ministry of caring for society.

An outright reversal of traditional positions of power

and importance is not intended. That is a wasteful game of competition. Rather the intention is to assume the most inclusive, fundamental perspective from which to view everything else. That perspective is the laity's, and it leads to a laicizing of ministry, taking as the norm what is normal for most Christians rather than taking as the norm what is least normal (ordination).

Love of the world, lay authority, engagement spirituality, occasion-centered community are only the merest hints of what might be implicated in a laicization of ministry as the care of society. As such, these suggestions stand as a kind of projection, an invitation to explore more fully what all this might mean and where it might take us.

What I see excites me; what I don't see humbles me; what I hope to see goes beyond this book.

# NOTES

## Introduction

1. Translation is the author's. The original text appears in *Acta Apostolicae Sedis,* 39 (1906) 8–9.
2. For the background and text of Newman's argument see John Coulson, *On Consulting the Faithful in Matters of Doctrine* (New York: Sheed and Ward, 1961). See also Jean Guitten, *The Church and the Laity* (Staten Island, N.Y.: Alba House, 1964).
3. The extent of Pius XI's treatment of Catholic Action is well known. See Arthur Alonzo, O.P., *Catholic Action and Laity* (St. Louis, Mo.: Herder Book Co., 1961); Jeremiah Newman, *What Is Catholic Action?* (Westminster, Md.: The Newman Press, 1958).
4. Yves Congar, *Lay People in the Church,* tr. Donald Attwater (Westminster, Md.: The Newman Press, 1957).
5. For a bibliography of significant preconciliar works see Rosemary Goldie, "Lay, Laity, Laicity: A Bibliographical Survey of Three Decades," in *Elements for a Theology of the Laity* (Vatican City: Vatican Press, 1979), pp. 107–144. See also Richard P. McBrien, "A Theology of the Laity," *The American Ecclesiastical Review* CLX (February 1968), pp. 73–86; Frederick Parrella, "The Laity in the Church," Catholic Theological Society of America *Proceedings* 35 (1980), pp. 264–287.

6. Andrew Greeley, Mary G. Durkin *et al., Parish, Priest, and People* (Chicago: The Thomas More Press, 1981), p. 169.

7. For a fuller explanation of this model, see Robert L. Kinast, "A Process Model of Theological Reflection," *The Journal of Pastoral Care* 37 (June 1983), pp. 144–156.

8. N.C.C.B., *Called and Gifted* (Washington, D.C.: USCC Publications Office, 1980).

## *Chapter One*

1. The stories of lay experience are found in many places, among them: *Gifts,* quarterly newsletter of the Bishops' Committee on the Laity (Washington, D.C.: USCC Publications Office); *St. Anthony Messenger* special issue on lay ministry, vol. 86 (March 1979), pp. 39–47; and Dennis Geaney, *Emerging Lay Ministries* (Kansas City, Mo.: Andrews and McMeel Inc., 1979).

2. For background literature on this section, see Eugene A. Walsh, S.S., *The Ministry of the Celebrating Community* (Glendale, Ariz.: Pastoral Arts Associates of North America, 1977); Joseph Champlin, *An Important Office of Immense Love* (Notre Dame, Ind.: Ave Maria Press, 1980); *Parish Development: Programs and Organizations* (Washington, D.C.: USCC Publications Office, 1980); Thomas P. Sweetser, S.J., *Successful Parishes* (Minneapolis, Minn.: Winston Press, 1984); William Rademacher, *Working with Parish Councils* (Canfield, Ohio: Alba Books, 1977); Judy Rauner, *Helping People Volunteer* (San Diego, Calif.: Marlborough Publishing Co., 1983); Robert Newsome, *The Ministering Parish* (Ramsey, N.J.: Paulist Press, 1982); Barbara Kuhn, *The*

*Whole Lay Ministry Catalogue* (New York: The Seabury Press, 1979).

3. For background literature on this section, see *Parish Life in the U.S.,* final report of the Parish Project (Washington, D.C.: USCC Publications Office, 1982); James Greer, "Problems of the Lay Minister as Role Initiator," in *Growing Together* (Washington, D.C.: USCC Publications Office, 1980), pp. 66–73; "What Are Pastoral Assistants in Germany?" *Origins* 10 (January 22, 1981), pp. 503–509.

4. For background literature on this section, see *Quest for Justice* (Washington, D.C.: USCC Publications Office, 1981); John A. Coleman, *An American Strategic Theology* (Ramsey, N.J.: Paulist Press, 1982); Herbert F. Weber, *The Parish Help Book* (Notre Dame, Ind.: Ave Maria Press, 1983); Mark Gibbs, *Christians with Secular Power* (Philadelphia: Fortress Press, 1981); *Salt,* a monthly magazine for those in grassroots social justice work published by Claretian Publications, Chicago, Ill.

5. Many of the characteristics of the dutiful Catholic parallel observations of Andrew Greeley in *The Communal Catholic* (New York: The Seabury Press, 1976).

6. For background literature on this section, see Dean R. Hoge, *Converts, Dropouts, Returnees* (New York: The Pilgrim Press, 1981); Mary G. Durkin and Andrew Greeley, *A Church to Come Home To* (Chicago: The Thomas More Press 1982); James Hug, ed., *Tracing the Spirit* (Ramsey, N.J.: Paulist Press, 1983); and a new service called Another Look: A National Ministry for the Inactive Catholic, sponsored by the Paulist Fathers' National Catholic Evangelization Association in Washington, D.C.

7. Yves Congar, O.P., "My Pathfindings in the Theology of Laity and Ministries," *The Jurist* 32 (Winter 1972), pp. 169–188.

8. Leonard Doohan, "Contemporary Theologies of the Laity," *Communio* 7 (1980), pp. 229–242.

9. The Chicago Declaration and major papers at the Notre Dame symposium are found in Russell Barta, *Challenge to the Laity* (Huntington, Ind.: Our Sunday Visitor Press, 1980).

10. *Called and Gifted,* already cited.

## Chapter Two

1. For background on the current discussion of ministry see John A. Coleman, "The Future of Ministry," *America* 144 (March 28, 1981), pp. 243–249; "Ministries in the Church: Symposium," *Chicago Studies* 16 (Summer 1977), pp. 163–259; James Dunning, *Ministries: Sharing God's Gifts* (Winona, Minn.: St. Mary's Press, 1980).

2. See "Asian Colloquium on Ministries: Conclusion," in *Origins* 8 (1978), pp. 129–143.

3. It is helpful to recall some critical views of the postconciliar church as found in James Hitchcock, *The Decline and Fall of Radical Catholicism* (New York: Herder and Herder, 1971); Peter Hebblethwaite, *The Runaway Church* (New York: The Seabury Press, 1975).

4. For background on the training of lay ministers, see Directory of Diocesan Lay Programs and Resources (Washington, D.C.: USCC Publications Office, 1981); Marian Schwab, "How Should We Train Lay Ministers?" *Ministries* 2 (March 1981), pp. 12–15. The National Association of Lay Ministry Coordinators is currently compiling an inventory of all types of lay training programs in the U.S.

## Chapter Three

1. For background on current lay-clergy relations, see Andrew Greeley, *The American Catholic: A Social Portrait* (New York: Basic Books, Inc., 1977), pp. 152–164. To get a little feeling for the way many lay persons experience themselves in relation to clergy, it may be a useful exercise to refer to the clergy as nonlaity. All the feeling associated with a negative description often accompanies the term laity.

2. One of the few extensive histories of the laity is the World Council of Churches study edited by Stephen Neill and Hans-Reudi Weber, *The Layman in Christian History* (Philadelphia: The Westminster Press, 1963). For a biblical history, see Francis O. Ayers, *The Ministry of the Laity: A Biblical Exposition* (Philadelphia: The Westminster Press, 1962). For a history of lay spirituality, see Gregory Widdowson, *An Outline of Lay Sanctity* (Huntington, Ind.: Our Sunday Visitor Press, 1979).

3. For background literature on this section, see David N. Power, O.M.I., *Gifts That Differ* (New York: The Pueblo Publishing Co., 1980); Edward Schillebeeckx, *Ministry* (New York: Crossroad Books, 1981); Thomas F. O'Meara, *Theology of Ministry* (Ramsey, N.J.: Paulist Press, 1983).

4. For background literature on this section, see John A. Coleman, *An American Strategic Theology* (Ramsey, N.J.: Paulist Press, 1982); Joseph Komonchak, "Clergy, Laity and the Church's Mission in the World," *The Jurist* 41 (1981), pp. 422–447; James and Evelyn Eaton Whitehead, *Community of Faith* (New York: The Seabury Press, 1982); George Peck and John S. Hoffman, eds. *The Laity in Ministry* (Valley Forge, PA: Judson, Press, 1984).

5. For background literature on this section, see *As One Who Serves* (Washington, D.C.: USCC Publications Office, 1977); *Program of Priestly Formation* (Washington, D.C.; USCC Publications Office, 1981); William J. Bausch, *Tradition, Tensions, Transitions in Ministry* (Mystic, Conn.: Twenty-Third Publications, 1982).

6. For background literature on this section, see Dennis Geaney, *Full Church, Empty Rectory* (Notre Dame, Ind.: Fides/Claretian, 1980); Howard W. Stone, *The Caring Church* (San Francisco: Harper & Row, 1983).

7. For a commentary on the church's modern social teaching, see David Hollenbach, S.J., *Claims in Conflict* (Ramsey, N.J.: Paulist Press, 1979); Francis Schüssler-Fiorenza, "The Social and Religious Mission of the Church," *Theological Studies* (1983).

8. On the secularity of the laity, a number of the works published during Vatican II are still very instructive, eg., Donald Thorman's *The Emerging Layman* (Garden City, N.Y.: Doubleday and Co. Inc., 1962). More recently, see Richard J. Mouw, *Called to Holy Worldliness* (Philadelphia: Fortress Press, 1980); Leonard Doohan, *The Lay-Centered Church* (Minneapolis, MN: Winston Press, 1984).

## Chapter Four

1. For background literature on this section, see C. W. Brister, *Pastoral Care in the Church* (New York: Harper & Row, 1977); Alaister Campbell, *Rediscovering Pastoral Care* (Philadelphia: The Westminister Press, 1981); William Arnold, *Introduction to Pastoral Care* (Nashville, Tenn.: Abingdon Press, 1982); Thomas Oden, *Pastoral Theology* (San Francisco: Harper & Row, 1983).

2. For some additional discussion of the notion of the care of society, see Robert L. Kinast, "Gaudium et Spes: The Pastoral Care of Society," *The Priest* 34 (July-August 1978), pp. 30–39; "Pastoral Care of Society as Liberation," *The Journal of Pastoral Care* 34 (June 1980), pp. 125–130; *Pastoral Care of Society,* audio cassette from New Life Films, Inc., Kansas City, Kans.